23917056

√6/00

WORLD
HISTORY SERIES

The
War of 1812

Titles in the World History Series

WORLD
HISTORY SERIES

The
War of 1812

by
Don Nardo

Lucent Books, P.O. Box 289011, San Diego, CA 92198-9011

Library of Congress Cataloging-in-Publication Data

Nardo, Don, 1947–
   The War of 1812 / by Don Nardo.
            p.   cm. — (World history series)
   Includes bibliographical references and index.
   Summary: Describes the War of 1812, including its prelude,
battles and campaigns, conclusion, and aftermath.
   ISBN 1-56006-581-8 (lib. : alk. paper)
   1. United States—History—War of 1812 Juvenile literature.
[1. United States—History—War of 1812.] I. Title. II. Series.
E354.N37 1999
973.5'2—dc21   99-14587
                                                               CIP

Copyright 2000 by Lucent Books, Inc., P.O. Box 289011,
San Diego, California 92198-9011

Printed in the U.S.A.

Contents

Foreword

Each year on the first day of school, nearly every history teacher faces the task of explaining why his or her students should study history. One logical answer to this question is that exploring what happened in our past explains how the things we often take for granted—our customs, ideas, and institutions—came to be. As statesman and historian Winston Churchill put it, "Every nation or group of nations has its own tale to tell. Knowledge of the trials and struggles is necessary to all who would comprehend the problems, perils, challenges, and opportunities which confront us today." Thus, a study of history puts modern ideas and institutions in perspective. For example, though the founders of the United States were talented and creative thinkers, they clearly did not invent the concept of democracy. Instead, they adapted some democratic ideas that had originated in ancient Greece and with which the Romans, the British, and others had experimented. An exploration of these cultures, then, reveals their very real connection to us through institutions that continue to shape our daily lives.

Another reason often given for studying history is the idea that lessons exist in the past from which contemporary societies can benefit and learn. This idea, although controversial, has always been an intriguing one for historians. Those who agree that society can benefit from the past often quote philosopher George Santayana's famous statement, "Those who cannot remember the past are condemned to repeat it." Historians who subscribe to Santayana's philosophy believe that, for example, studying the events that led up to the major world wars or other significant historical events would allow society to chart a different and more favorable course in the future.

Just as difficult as convincing students to realize the importance of studying history is the search for useful and interesting supplementary materials that present historical events in a context that can be easily understood. The volumes in Lucent Books' World History Series attempt to present a broad, balanced, and penetrating view of the march of history. Ancient Egypt's important wars and rulers, for example, are presented against the rich and colorful backdrop of Egyptian religious, social, and cultural developments. The series engages the reader by enhancing historical events with these cultural contexts. For example, in *Ancient Greece,* the text covers the role of women in that society. Slavery is discussed in *The Roman Empire,* as well as how slaves earned their freedom. The numerous and varied aspects of every-day life in these and other societies are explored in each volume of the series. Additionally, the series covers the major political, cultural, and philosophical ideas as the torch of civilization is passed from ancient Mesopotamia and Egypt, through Greece, Rome, Medieval Europe, and other world cultures, to the modern day.

The material in the series is formatted in a thorough, precise, and organized manner. Each volume offers the reader a comprehensive and clearly written overview of an important historical event or period. The topic under discussion is placed in a broad, historical context. For example, *The Italian Renaissance* begins with a discussion of the High Middle Ages and the loss of central control that allowed certain Italian cities to develop artistically. The book ends by looking forward to the Reformation and interpreting the societal changes that grew out of the Renaissance. Thus, students are not only involved in an historical era, but also enveloped by the events leading up to that era and the events following it.

One important and unique feature in the World History Series is the primary and secondary source quotations that richly supplement each volume. These quotes are useful in a number of ways. First, they allow students access to sources they would not normally be exposed to because of the difficulty and obscurity of the original source. The quotations range from interesting anecdotes to far-sighted cultural perspectives and are drawn from historical witnesses both past and present. Second, the quotes demonstrate how and where historians themselves derive their information on the past as they strive to reach a consensus on historical events. Lastly, all of the quotes are footnoted, familiarizing students with the citation process and allowing them to verify quotes and/or look up the original source if the quote piques their interest.

Finally, the books in the World History Series provide a detailed launching point for further research. Each book contains a bibliography specifically geared toward student research. A second, annotated bibliography introduces students to all the sources the author consulted when compiling the book. A chronology of important dates gives students an overview, at a glance, of the topic covered. Where applicable, a glossary of terms is included.

In short, the series is designed not only to acquaint readers with the basics of history, but also to make them aware that their lives are a part of an ongoing human saga. Perhaps they will then come to the same realization as famed historian Arnold Toynbee. In his monumental work, *A Study of History,* he wrote about becoming aware of history flowing through him in a mighty current, and of his own life "welling like a wave in the flow of this vast tide."

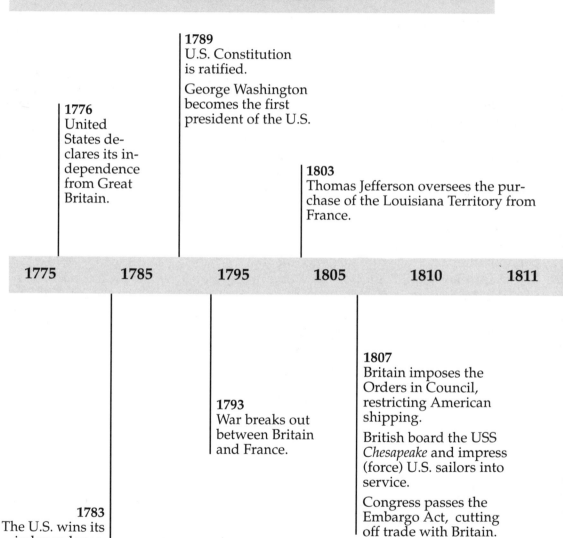

IMPORTANT DATES IN THE HISTORY OF THE WAR OF 1812

1789
U.S. Constitution is ratified.

George Washington becomes the first president of the U.S.

1776
United States declares its independence from Great Britain.

1803
Thomas Jefferson oversees the purchase of the Louisiana Territory from France.

| 1775 | 1785 | 1795 | 1805 | 1810 | 1811 |

1807
Britain imposes the Orders in Council, restricting American shipping.

British board the USS *Chesapeake* and impress (force) U.S. sailors into service.

Congress passes the Embargo Act, cutting off trade with Britain.

1793
War breaks out between Britain and France.

1783
The U.S. wins its independence.

1812

June 18: The U.S. formally declares war on Britain.

July 16–19: USS *Constitution* outruns a squadron of British ships.

August 16: Americans in Fort Detroit surrender.

August 19: The *Constitution* attacks the British warship *Guerriere.*

1813

September 10: Perry defeats the British on Lake Erie.

October 5: Harrison defeats British and Indian forces on the Thames River in Canada.

1815

January 8: Andrew Jackson leads Americans to a decisive victory over the British outside New Orleans.

February 17: President James Madison declares the War of 1812 to be officially over.

| 1811 | 1812 | 1813 | 1814 | 1815 | 1816 |

1811
William Henry Harrison defeats the Prophet at Tippecanoe Creek.

1814
March 27: Andrew Jackson defeats Creek Indians at Horseshoe Bend in Alabama.

August 24: British capture and burn Washington, D.C.

September 13: British bombard Fort McHenry outside Baltimore.

December 24: Americans and British sign Treaty of Ghent in Belgium.

Introduction

A War Scarcely Anyone Wanted

President Harry S Truman called the War of 1812 "the silliest damn war we ever had."[1] Other common phrases that have been used over the years to describe the second and last military conflict between the United States and Great Britain include "unnecessary," "impractical," and "pointless." As far back as the war's outbreak, one of the warring parties thought the other's grievances were far too trivial to fight over. When the news arrived in Britain that the United States had declared war, the British, leaders and average citizens alike, were shocked and perplexed. In August 1812 the *Examiner,* a popular London newspaper, echoed the opinion of most British when it stated, "If the Father of evil himself had planned this mischief, he could not have contrived a rupture more hateful to humanity, or one more destitute of the most remote advantage to any body."[2] Many Americans agreed. The war was generally unpopular in the United States, and particularly so in the New England states, which after two years of fighting seemed almost on the verge of seceding from the Union.

Indeed, unlike most other wars fought by the Americans and British against various foes, the War of 1812 was not declared in response to an armed attack or other serious confrontation. There was no Pearl Harbor or sinking of the *Maine* to inflame national passions and justify sending troops into battle. Instead, the War of 1812 was the result of a steady buildup of tensions between the two nations. Over the course of several years, the United States and Britain squabbled about British mistreatment of American sailors, British friendship with Native Americans, and trade policies and taxes. With a sincere effort from both sides, most of these relatively minor disputes might have been resolved through peaceful means. But neither side made that effort. And once hostilities commenced, the initial bloodshed caused mutual tensions and hatreds to increase and the war to escalate. As Canadian scholar Pierre Berton puts it, the conflict was "a foolish war that scarcely anyone wanted or needed, but which, once launched, none knew how to stop."[3]

Add to these facts another telling one: Given the huge territories and great distances involved, the whole enterprise was impractical to begin with. The British were used to fighting within the relatively compact, connected, and familiar lands of Europe. By contrast, a war with the

United States required maintaining supply lines across the vast Atlantic Ocean and marching armies through unfamiliar wilderness more than twice the size of Europe. Moreover, transportation and communications were extremely primitive by today's standards. Travel by foot, horse, and ship was slow and tedious, and armies took weeks, sometimes even months, to move from one strategic point to another. Commanders on both sides of the conflict were out of touch with their superiors for long periods of time, making it extremely difficult to coordinate military operations effectively. And it took so long for news to cross the ocean that important documents that might have prevented much of the bloodshed did not reach their destination in time.

It must also be emphasized that both sides made some serious mistakes in prosecuting the war. The United States was particularly guilty of "bungling and mismanagement," writes noted historian Donald Hickey.

> This was partly due to the nature of the republic. The nation was too young and immature—and its government too feeble and inexperienced— to

The grave of a Connecticut man who served in the War of 1812 gives no indication of the pointlessness of the conflict, in which the U.S. and Britain clashed over relatively minor grievances.

prosecute a major war efficiently. Politics also played a part. . . . Even those who supported the war feuded among themselves and never displayed the sort of patriotic enthusiasm that has been so evident in other American wars. The advocates of war appeared to support the conflict more with their heads than their hearts, and more with their hearts than their purses. As a result, efforts to raise men and money lagged far behind need.[4]

Another factor that made the War of 1812 both unusual and pointless was the ultimate lack of a clear winner. Each side won its share of victories. But neither nation decisively defeated the other, and the conflict concluded in a political stalemate. The peace treaty the combatants signed avoided addressing their grievances and served merely to bring an official end to the fighting. Considering all of these factors, historian George R. Taylor sums up the consensus of modern scholarship this way:

> [The war's] causes were unclear at the time and remain to this day the subject of lively dispute. The conduct of the war on land proved almost incredibly incompetent and blunder-

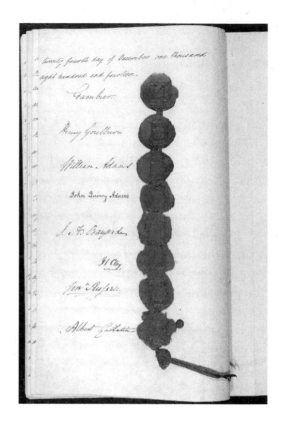

Signatures and wax seals adorn the Treaty of Ghent, signed on December 24, 1814, a document that failed to address the war's causes.

ing. And the conflict ended in a treaty of peace which failed to mention the chief issues which were alleged to have contributed to its beginning.[5]

1 Down the Fateful Road to War

In 1800, the English-speaking peoples on both sides of the Atlantic Ocean were optimistic about the new century. The British hoped that their already formidable empire would expand and bring them even more wealth and power. The many British colonies around the globe were part of an impressive trade network that made Great Britain the economic giant of its day. With a population of 16 million, Britain maintained a large standing army, often numbering more than 100,000 men, and the world's biggest and most advanced navy, making it one of the most powerful nations on earth.

The new century also seemed promising for the citizens of the infant United States. With a population of only 5 million, a standing army of fewer than four thousand men, and a tiny navy, the new nation was not an important military power. Yet it controlled huge and diverse territories filled with untapped natural resources. The U.S. had many fine harbors on the Atlantic coastline, millions of acres of rich farmland, and vast forests and plains on its southern and western frontiers. This natural wealth increased considerably when, on May 2, 1803, President Thomas Jefferson bought the Louisiana Territory from France for just $15 million. Encompassing an area of more than 800,000 square miles, the new territory almost doubled the size of the U.S. overnight, making the country's potential for future development and expansion seem nearly endless.

OLD TENSIONS LINGER AND INCREASE

But while both the British and Americans optimistically faced the challenges and opportunities of the new century, tensions from the old century lingered. Remembering their recent fight for independence, many Americans still resented and disliked the British. In their view, the British social and political system was corrupt, in large part because it seemed to be controlled by self-serving aristocrats who cared little for the common people. To most Americans, the British kings and queens seemed tyrannical or at least part of an outdated form of government, one inferior to the new American democratic system.

THE UNITED STATES IN 1812

When the Americans and British began fighting in 1812, the United States was already a large country. There were eighteen states—the original thirteen, plus five that had entered the Union after 1790: Vermont (admitted in 1791), Kentucky (1792), Tennessee (1796), Ohio (1803), and Louisiana, which joined the Union less than two months before the United States declared war in June 1812.

In addition to the states, the country claimed ownership of several large territories, including, for example, the region encompassed by what are now the states of Mississippi and Alabama. The largest U.S. territory at the time was Missouri, made up of most of the lands of the vast former Louisiana Territory, purchased from France in 1803 by Thomas Jefferson's first administration. These rolling plains and hills would later become the states of Arkansas, Missouri, Iowa, Nebraska, Kansas, and South Dakota, as well as parts of Texas, Oklahoma, Colorado, and Wyoming. In 1812, U.S. territories were sparsely settled by both Indians and whites.

Including the states and territories, the United States then stretched north-south from New Hampshire to the Gulf of Mexico, and east-west from the Atlantic Ocean to the Great Plains. This huge expanse covered more than 1.68 million square miles, an area about seventeen times larger than Great Britain. In 1812, most U.S. forests, valleys, and river systems, whose natural riches would eventually help to make the country wealthy and prosperous, were still largely unexplored and undeveloped by whites.

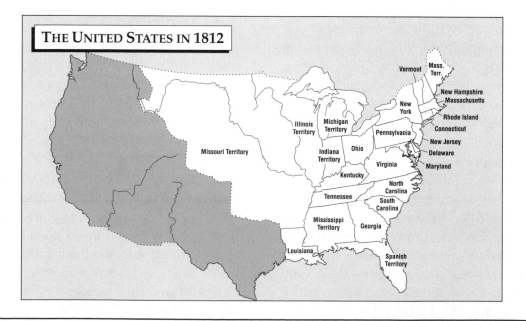

THE UNITED STATES IN 1812

By contrast, most British citizens were still angry and unhappy about losing the American colonies. The British tended to view Americans as undisciplined and uncultured upstarts and American democracy as a form of "mob rule" that was sure to eventually collapse into chaos. Many in Britain believed that, sooner or later, the former colonies would once again come under Britain's sway.

These and other old problems between the two nations seemed to worsen rather than improve as time went on. During and following the American Revolution, there had been border disputes between the United States and British-controlled Canada. A boundary settlement in 1783 did not specify the exact border, and each side claimed some of the same pieces of land. Also, the British sought to hold on to many of their forts and outposts along the Great Lakes, around which most Canadians lived at that time. In addition, the British attempted to claim territory in the Ohio Valley, Kentucky, and other areas of the frontier in order to retain control over the valuable fur trade, as well as the local Indians who were Britain's military allies.

To strengthen their position, the British tried to discourage American settlers from entering these areas. To accomplish this, British military commanders encouraged many of the Indian tribes to harass and attack the settlers, which in turn caused many Americans to hate and distrust nearly all Indians. As Levi Todd, an officer in the Kentucky militia, described in a March 1788 letter to the governor of the territory, the following series of assaults was typical:

King George III of England. Americans viewed the British monarchy as outdated and corrupt.

The Indians . . . have discovered a disposition to prosecute a war against us with uncommon ardor [eagerness] and usual barbarity. . . . They have repeatedly fired upon the inhabitants of these counties and several have been killed. Last week they made an attack on the house of Mr. Shank on the frontier . . . in the night. They killed five of his family, destroyed the property, and burnt the house. This [being] but too common, they escaped without adequate punishment. . . . The inhabitants on the frontier of each of these counties are alarmed and . . . it is hard to say where the evil will terminate.[6]

A British soldier trades a gun to an Indian in exchange for American scalps. In fact, the British regularly encouraged the Indians to attack American settlers.

Since the Americans knew full well who had inspired the attacks, these incidents also sparked hatred and resentment of the British. Undeterred, however, American settlers continued to pour into the frontier. Between 1783 and 1812, for example, the population of Kentucky increased from 12,000 to 400,000, and by 1810 more than 230,000 Americans had settled in the Ohio Valley. Not surprisingly, as the British continued to incite Indian attacks against the settlers, tensions steadily increased.

MARITIME DISPUTES AND JAY'S TREATY

There was certainly resentment among the British, too. After the Revolution, the two countries became trade rivals, and because Britain wanted to maintain its mastery of the global sea trade, it passed laws designed to keep American ships from trading with British colonies and allies around the world. But during the 1780s and 1790s, Americans found ways to get around these laws. For instance, many American merchants docked and traded at small ports that were not regularly visited and policed by the British navy, while others traded with nations that were close neighbors of British colonies. These "neutral" parties shuffled goods back and forth between U.S. ships and British markets. Such manipulative maneuvers angered many British, especially in the wealthy classes, who viewed American competition as a threat to Britain's economy.

Complicating matters further, in 1793 Britain went to war against its longtime rival, France. The British blockaded French ports, destroyed French ships, and issued a decree vowing that Britain would seize any foreign ships trying to trade with the French. This placed the United States in a difficult position because its trade with France and the many French colonies around the world was important to the American economy. Americans were also understandably angry that the British had tried to keep the United States out of Britain's markets and now attempted to exclude it from French markets as well. Seeing no other choice, large numbers of American merchants violated the British decree and carried on a booming trade with the French.

In retaliation, the British confiscated more than 250 American ships, a series of acts that outraged the American public. The British also boarded many U.S. vessels at will to search for British deserters. Oftentimes, they took advantage of such boarding incidents to impress, or force, American sailors into serving in the British navy instead. This practice was motivated largely by the fact that thousands of British sailors, sick of the terrible living conditions on most British ships, had for some time been deserting these vessels to take jobs on American vessels. In a later indignant condemnation of impressment, the *National Intelligencer*, a major U.S. newspaper, printed the following description of the practice:

A British officer attempts to persuade a group of Indians to become allies of Britain and fight against the Americans.

When [American] vessels are met with on the ocean by British vessels of war; on being boarded, a demand is made of *the roll*, or articles, and the men being mustered [assembled], the [British] officer interrogates them . . . to decide and determine the place of birth of every man on board. . . . The fate of the men being thus summarily decided, *the condemned* are taken on board the [British] man of war. . . . Melancholy prospect, worst of slavery, *to fight for their oppressors!* . . . At length they listen to the seductive *hope of opportunity to regain their liberty* . . . but double disappointment follows; the ship goes into port, and they find themselves more strictly watched![7]

A number of outraged U.S. officials demanded war with Britain over the shipping disputes and the impressment issue. But President George Washington realized that the United States was unprepared for a full-scale war and wisely attempted to avoid a conflict. He sent Chief Justice John Jay to negotiate with the British in 1794. Knowing that their superior military strength gave them the advantage in the talks, the British forced Jay to accept a settlement that, at least on the surface, seemed heavily to favor Britain and its interests. For example, according to the treaty the British agreed not to confiscate any more American ships, but the Americans could no longer trade with the French and were still excluded from most British markets.

Learning of these seemingly lopsided terms, many Americans, especially prominent members of the Republican Party (the opposing party to Washington's Federalists, then in power), called the treaty a "sellout" to the British. And in the streets angry mobs burned straw dummies marked with Jay's name. (These reactions were in large part unjustified. Although Jay had made little headway in solving the maritime disputes, he had managed to avert war and also to prevent the British from gaining important concessions on the Canadian border, the Mississippi River, and other parts of the frontier. Such

A British naval officer indicates that an American sailor is to be impressed, against his will, into British service.

President George Washington sent Chief Justice John Jay (pictured) to negotiate with the British over shipping disputes and impressment.

concessions would have given Britain a firm foothold in the Midwest and prevented later U.S. westward expansion.) In fact, the treaty did not stop the British from harassing American vessels; in the following years relations between the two nations remained strained.

THE *CHESAPEAKE* INCIDENT AND JEFFERSON'S EMBARGO

As the nineteenth century dawned, renewed conflict between Britain and France once more caused problems for the United States. After nearly a decade of fighting, the British and French signed a peace treaty in 1802, but only a year later hostilities erupted again between the two countries. In 1804, Napoleon Bonaparte, military dictator of France, prepared for

a large-scale invasion of Britain, and French ships challenged Britain's control of the seas. As tensions increased, each side claimed the right to seize any foreign ships daring to deal with its enemy. The United States, by now the world's largest neutral trading nation, was once more caught in a dilemma, for no matter which side it traded with, it risked losing ships and sailors.

The situation further deteriorated in 1807 when the British enacted the Orders in Council. These were rules that forbade any neutral nation from trading with any European nation except through British ports and with British licenses. The rules were designed to accomplish two goals. First, Britain wanted to cut off the flow of goods into French-controlled sections of Europe. Second, forcing U.S. and other foreign merchants to trade strictly through British ports would greatly help Britain's economy. Once more, a majority of Americans expressed outrage. Accordingly, many American ships defiantly refused to get licenses and evaded British and French blockades, some sneaking through under the cover of darkness, others resorting to bribery and outright smuggling.

Meanwhile, the British continued to seize U.S. ships and to impress American sailors. The most notorious such incident occurred in June 1807 when, only ten minutes after sailing from Norfolk, Virginia, the U.S. warship *Chesapeake* encountered the British warship *Leopard*. Per the usual seizure and impressment procedure, the British captain demanded the right to examine the *Chesapeake*'s crew. He had reason to believe that a British deserter

BRITISH WARSHIPS BANNED FROM U.S. WATERS

The following excerpt (quoted in volume 1 of Dudley's Naval War of 1812) *is from President Thomas Jefferson's July 2, 1807, proclamation expelling British warships from American waters. This was in response to the seizure of and attack on the American vessel* Chesapeake *by the British ship* Leopard *about ten days before.*

"During the wars which, for some time, have unhappily prevailed among the powers of Europe; the United States of America, firm in their principles of peace, have endeavored. . . to maintain, with all the belligerents [warring parties], their accustomed relations of friendship. . . . A free use of their harbors and waters. . . have, at all times, and on equal principles, been extended to all. . . amidst a constant recurrence of acts of. . . violence to the persons, [and] of trespasses on the property of our citizens, committed by officers of one of the belligerent parties [i.e., Britain]. . . . At length a deed, transcending [worse than] all we have hitherto seen or suffered, brings the public sensibility to a serious crisis. . . . A frigate of the U.S. trusting to a state of peace. . . has been surprised and attacked by a British vessel of superior force. . . with the loss of a number of men killed and wounded. This enormity was not only without provocation or justifiable cause, but was committed with the avowed purpose of taking by force. . . a part of her crew. . . . In consideration of these circumstances and the right of every nation to. . . provide for its peace & for the safety of its citizens. . . I have thought proper. . . to issue this Proclamation, hereby requiring all armed vessels bearing commissions under the government of Great Britain, now within the harbors or waters of the U.S. immediately & without delay to depart from the same."

A U.S. sailor struggles in vain to escape the British seamen who drag him toward their warship.

named Jenkin Ratford, who had publicly denounced the British, was aboard. The captain of the American ship, James Barron, was furious, largely because this was the first time that the British had tried to take seamen from a naval warship (all former incidents involved merchant ships). Angrily, Barron refused the British demand; in response, the *Leopard* blasted the *Chesapeake* with its cannon. Because the *Chesapeake* was unprepared for combat, it could not retaliate and suffered heavy damage, forcing Barron to give in. Several British officers boarded the crippled ship and seized Ratford, as well as three American sailors.

Fuming over the incident, a number of members of the U.S. Congress demanded an immediate war declaration against Britain. But these "war hawks," as they came to be called, were not yet in the majority, and most U.S. lawmakers backed the Republican president, Thomas Jefferson, who had what he believed was a better alternative to war. First, he expelled British warships from U.S. waters; then, intending to teach both Britain and France a lesson, he cut off trade with them and also with the countries that traded with them. This second maneuver, he reasoned, would hurt them financially and thereby force them to come to terms with the United States. In December 1807, Congress passed Jefferson's Embargo Act, which kept American ships bound for any foreign nation from leaving U.S. ports.

But the embargo was a failure. Rather than being hurt by it, the British actually profited by taking over the share of foreign trade that the Americans had given up. At the same time, the overall loss of trade severely damaged the American economy, and the British, maintaining their Orders in Council, continued impressing American seamen. In 1809, just before leaving office, Jefferson lifted the embargo. But the damage had been done, for American merchants continued to suffer and the United States appeared weak and powerless in the eyes of the European powers.

ECONOMIC EFFECTS IN VARIOUS U.S. REGIONS

It must be emphasized that, although most of the United States suffered financially from the effects of Jefferson's embargo, a few parts of the country actually profited. Some U.S. merchants, particularly those living in the New England states where smuggling was already widespread, ignored the rules and became rich by conducting illegal, secret trade with foreign nations. They also made special deals with the British and continued to receive British goods and money. The British made these deals hoping to get New England to break away from the United States and ally itself with Britain.

The fact was that few New Englanders wanted war with Britain. They were furious over the embargo and opposed many U.S. policies so strongly that many of them claimed to feel more British than American. Congressmen from the region argued that a war with Britain would totally ruin the U.S. economy. They insisted that the United States and Britain should settle their differences peacefully; and to press home their point, some New England states threatened to secede from the Union rather than fight.

But many people in other parts of the country were not so convinced that Britain would listen to reason and respond to American grievances. Although the American embargo had been lifted, the British Orders in Council had not, and they continued to restrict U.S. shipping. The resultant loss of trade inflicted economic hardships on the American South, the region stretching from Virginia southward to Georgia and the Mississippi Territory. Farmers found increasingly fewer markets for their crops, and many southerners lost their jobs. The West, including Ohio, Tennessee, and Kentucky, also suffered, as thousands of western farmers, having no one to buy their grain, sat on huge surpluses and faced financial ruin. In 1810, large sections of the South and West experienced an economic depression, and public support for the war hawks, who came mainly from these areas, steadily grew.

The country's economic troubles became even worse after James Madison succeeded Jefferson as president. Desiring to keep as much pressure on Britain as they could, the French tricked Madison into reinstating the embargo late in 1810. Napoleon led Madison to believe that the French would lift their own restrictions against U.S. shipping if the Americans resumed the embargo against Britain, but the French did not keep their part of the bargain. Nevertheless, Madison stubbornly maintained the embargo, continuing to hope that it would eventually hurt the British enough to force them to suspend the Orders in Council.

ATTACKS ON THE FRONTIER

While Americans continued to endure British shipping restrictions and confrontations at sea, American-British disputes along the frontier began to heat up. Britain increased its efforts to arm the Indians and to incite them against American settlers. In 1810, Indian attacks escalated into full-scale warfare between whites and pro-British tribes such as the Shawnee and Potawatomi. The most prominent Native American leader in the region, the great Shawnee chief Tecumseh, felt that he had good reason to ally himself with the British against the Americans. As a young man, he had seen his father and elder brothers killed while resisting white settlers who had seized some Shawnee lands. An intelligent and skilled leader, Tecumseh foresaw that the whites would eventually take over all Indian lands, and he preached that all tribes must stand together against the increasing flood of American settlers. Practicing what he preached, he dedicated himself to attempting to unite the tribes of the northwestern frontier into a single, strong alliance.

In November 1811, responding to Tecumseh's attacks on American settlements in the Indiana Territory, William Henry Harrison, that territory's recently appointed governor, moved on the Indians.

James Madison (left), the fourth U.S. president, reinstated the embargo partly at the urging of France's dictator, Napoleon Bonaparte (right), who hoped it would inflict economic damage on the British.

Leading a force of some nine hundred troops, Harrison camped near Tippecanoe Creek, in northern Indiana. Across the creek stood a large village commanded by Tecumseh's brother, Tenskwatawa, commonly known as the Prophet, an individual with few leadership skills whose authority rested mainly on his supposed ability to see into the future. On the evening of November 6, he chanted before a huge bonfire, then told his followers that he had cast a spell over the American camp. "One half of the white chief's army is now dead," he claimed. "The other half is now crazy. It will be a small matter to finish them off with our tomahawks."[8]

Early in the cold, rainy morning of November 7, the Prophet led more than two thousand warriors through the woods toward Harrison's camp. After an American sentry spotted them and opened fire, they attacked. Hearing the sound of musket fire, Harrison, who was getting dressed, ran from his tent and jumped onto his aide's horse by mistake, while the aide mounted Harrison's horse, a gray mare. This seemingly trivial mistake actually saved the governor's life, for a few minutes later the aide was killed by Indians who, seeing him on the gray mare, mistook him for Harrison.

Normally the Indians would have moved forward cautiously, taking advantage of

An artist's depiction of the Battle of Tippecanoe. Acting on the misguided advice of Prophet, the Indians rushed headlong into the American lines and certain death.

the cover of rocks and trees. But the Prophet had foretold that the whites were nearly defenseless, so his warriors charged in the open, running headlong at the American lines. In blazes of musket fire, the white soldiers drove them back three times. By this time, the attacking warriors had deduced that the whites were not all dead or insane, as their leader had promised; at the same time they noticed that the Prophet had deserted them and fled, so they swiftly retreated. Later that day, the victorious Harrison ordered the Indian village burned to the ground.

The incident at Tippecanoe significantly increased tensions between the United States and the British-Indian alliance. Tecumseh, enraged by his brother's defeat, firmly sided with the British, who supplied the Indians with more arms than ever and urged them to continue their attacks on the settlers. This further outraged Americans. The Lexington *Reporter* voiced the feelings of many when it asked if Congress intended to "treat the citizens of the *Western country* as they have treated the [harassed and impressed] seaman"[9] for eighteen years? And the *Aurora*, a Philadelphia paper, angrily declared that "war has been begun with British arms and by the Indians instigated by British emissaries. The blood of American citizens has already been shed in actual war, begun undeclared."[10]

This increasingly hostile national mood played directly into the hands of the congressional war hawks. They not only demanded war to maintain the nation's honor but wanted the United States to invade Canada, which, they said, would remove British influence from the northwestern frontier once and for all. Though they did not admit it openly, the hawks saw taking Canada as only the first step toward a larger goal. Along with many other Americans, they believed that as their nation's population grew, new territories would be needed to accommodate it. To some, it seemed inevitable that the United States would eventually come to control all of North America; and at the moment the main obstacle to achieving this goal was Britain, which desperately wanted to retain a foothold on the continent. Therefore, the hawks reasoned, fighting and defeating the British would conveniently clear the way for American expansion.

THE WAR HAWKS WIN THE DAY

No single event, therefore, brought the two countries to the brink of war; rather, from the American vantage it seemed that numerous maritime and frontier disputes and outrages had piled up for almost three decades, severely straining the nation's patience. Growing numbers of Americans felt helpless and wanted the government to take a stand, even if it meant going down the fateful road to war. As long as the hawks' opponents controlled Congress, however, there could be no war.

What finally made a war declaration a viable possibility was the outcome of the national elections of 1811. Voters in the South and West, sick of their economic woes and the British-inspired Indian threat, elected to Congress about forty influential war hawks, who made the prowar faction a majority for the first time. This group was led by Kentucky's forceful and energetic Henry Clay, who was elected to the powerful post of Speaker of the House of Representatives. This gave him the power to appoint hawks as heads of important committees, including those controlling foreign relations, military affairs, and the navy. Now, every British insult, no matter how small, was enthusiastically denounced in Congress.

As Speaker of the House of Representatives, Henry Clay led the war hawk faction, a group that wanted to go to war with Britain.

PRESIDENT MADISON CALLS FOR WAR

On June 1, 1812, President James Madison delivered to Congress a declaration outlining U.S. grievances against Britain (excerpted here from Taylor's War of 1812).

"Without going back beyond the renewal in 1803 of the war in which Great Britain is engaged [with France], and omitting unrepaired wrongs of inferior magnitude, the conduct of her Government presents a series of acts hostile to the United States as an independent and neutral nation. British cruisers have been in the continued practice of violating the American flag on the great highway of nations, and of seizing and carrying off persons sailing under it. . . . British cruisers have been in the practice also of violating the rights and the peace of our coasts. They hover over and harass our entering and departing commerce. To the most insulting pretensions they have added the most lawless proceedings in our very harbors, and have wantonly spilt American blood within the sanctuary of our territorial jurisdiction [authority]. . . . Under pretended blockades . . . our commerce has been plundered in every sea, the great staples of our country have been cut off from their legitimate markets, and a destructive blow aimed at our agricultural and maritime interests. Not content with . . . laying waste our neutral trade . . . Britain resorted at length to the sweeping system of blockades, under the name Orders in Council, which has been molded and managed as might best suit its political views. . . . Whether the United States shall continue passive under these . . . accumulating wrongs . . . is a solemn question which the Constitution wisely confides to the legislative department of the government [i.e., only Congress has the authority to declare war]. In recommending it [war] to their early deliberations I am happy in the assurance that the decision will be worthy of the enlightened and patriotic councils of a virtuous, a free, and a powerful nation."

In this volatile atmosphere, the hawks convinced Madison to demand that the British cancel their Orders in Council, which still restricted U.S. shipping; the president did so, sending a written message on a vessel sailing for Britain. But when there was no immediate response, a majority of American leaders decided it was time to fight. On June 1, 1812, Madison delivered his war message to Congress, reciting the litany of British offenses, including the violation of "the American flag on the great highway of nations, and the seizing and carrying off of persons sailing under it." American goods, he said, had "been cut off from their legitimate markets, and a destructive blow aimed at our agricultural and maritime interests." Furthermore, there was "the warfare just renewed by the savages on one of our extensive frontiers—a warfare which is known to spare neither age nor sex and to be distinguished by features peculiarly shocking to humanity."[11] The House passed the declaration by a vote of 79 to 49 on June 4, and the Senate passed it by 19 to 13 votes on June 17.

What American leaders did not know during these stormy, fateful deliberations was that the British had finally begun to give in to U.S. pressure and demands. By the early months of 1812, Madison's embargo had actually started working, causing British merchants to feel their economic pinch and motivating many British politicians to call for the removal of the Orders in Council. The Orders in Council were repealed on June 16. But because news of the event, like Madison's earlier message, had to travel on sailing ships over a great distance, it did not reach the United States until it was too late. On June 18, the day after the Senate's approval of the war declaration and two days after the British had removed the major obstacle to peace, the United States formally declared war on Britain. Clay and his war hawks had won the day. But the large and worried minority of Americans who opposed them wondered if the nation could win the war.

2 The Disastrous Canadian Campaign

In the summer of 1812, the United States was officially at war with one of the world's great powers. The president, members of Congress, and military leaders all agreed that their best chance was to defeat the British on land. The British navy was far more powerful than the tiny U.S. fleet, and the Americans were convinced that there was virtually no chance for a victory at sea. So U.S. leaders unanimously decided to attack and capture the British-Canadian forts and towns in the Great Lakes region, the so-called Old Northwest, which was where British power in North America was most concentrated.

By contrast, the American presence in the region was sparse. According to military historian John Elting, in 1812, U.S. interests in the Old Northwest were rather weakly guarded

> by a thin screen of stockaded forts, most of which also were government trading posts, or "factories." Their tiny, often sickly garrisons [defending forces] were merely symbols of the United States' territorial claims, pushed out into the far reaches of the frontier to fend for themselves. Detroit, the key post of the Old Northwest, had a garrison of some 120 regulars [i.e., full-time soldiers, as opposed to part-time militiamen]; Fort Mackinac [in northern Michigan] . . . had 62; Fort Dearborn (modern Chicago) 50-odd. Another 50 men or so garrisoned Fort Madison, on the west bank of the Mississippi. . . . Further east, Fort Wayne—another frontier post that would become a city—had approximately 85 regulars. . . . Fort Harrison, built by [William Henry] Harrison in 1811 near modern Terre Haute on his way to Tippecanoe, might have had 50 more.[12]

Because the region was so thinly settled, very few local militiamen were available to reinforce these frontier posts. But in the view of American leaders, this weakness could easily be overcome by sending an army of regulars into the area. Using the forts as strategic bases, they would conquer Canada, an operation that promised to remove the British from the continent and at the same time expand the size of the United States considerably.

At first, many Americans were confident, and some even expressed open enthusiasm, that an attack on Canada could not fail. One obvious factor in the Americans' favor was that Canada's population was only about 500,000, roughly one-fifteenth that of the United States. Although the American standing army was very small, the country's large population seemed to guarantee a ready and ample pool from which to raise more troops. Other U.S. advantages were that the British had to defend a border some seventeen hundred miles long with fewer than eight thousand troops and that they would receive few reinforcements, since most of Britain's huge standing army was occupied with fighting Napoleon in Europe. And although the British had thousands of Indian allies, American military officers were sure that their army could easily defeat the Indians, whom most Americans regarded as undisciplined savages. As proof of American superiority over the Indians, many cited Harrison's recent decisive victory at Tippecanoe.

AN ARMY BESET BY PROBLEMS

But in reality, the United States was no more prepared to fight a major land war than it was a naval one. The naked truth was that the American military had so many weaknesses and problems that its proposed conquest of Canada was doomed from the start. To begin with, as Temple University scholar Russell Weigley explains, in 1812 the United States had

> little more existing military strength or military administrative machinery than in 1775. The regular Army of something under 7,000 was not only small, but . . . any advantage [it] represented in the military situation of 1812 over 1775 was largely cancelled out by the tendency, if not necessity, to continue scattering it across the long Canadian border and Indian frontier and along a coastline that now reached to the mouth of the

An old engraving depicts an American fort overlooking the Great Lakes. In 1812, most such outposts, like Fort Detroit and Fort Dearborn, were manned by only 50 to 120 regular soldiers.

Mississippi. A sustained war effort would again have to be built, as in the Revolution, upon volunteer militia companies.[13]

There were, in fact, about fifty thousand militiamen, mostly farmers and merchants, who could be called up to fight during an emergency. But the problem was that the militias were under the command of the state governors, who refused to enter the national fight until their respective states were attacked. For the Canadian campaign, therefore, the federal government had to make do with the small regular army.

One of that army's glaring weaknesses was a serious morale problem. Many of the soldiers did not really want a military career and had signed up for only a year or so to see what being in the army was like. Quite often, they decided that they hated military life and then talked about little else but going home. During the late 1700s and early 1800s, it was not unusual for soldiers to pack up and leave when their term of enlistment was over, even on the eve of an important battle when they were sorely needed.

Supply problems certainly contributed to this poor morale. Transporting tons of supplies to distant armies across hundreds of thousands of square miles of untamed wilderness was extremely difficult at the time and sometimes outright impossible. In addition, there was often not enough money in the U.S. Treasury to pay for the huge amounts of supplies needed, at which times the troops were forced to do without adequate food and clothing. "The American clothing industry" itself, writes Weigley, "was still an infant despite forced-draft growth under embargoes and war, and the quality of uniforms . . . remained low. Shoes were described as made of leather 'as porous as a sponge.'"[14]

Adding to the army's manpower and morale problems was its lack of strong, vigorous leadership. According to Weigley:

> Its senior officers were men of little talent. The older regiments were still commanded by aging Revolutionary veterans; the regiments raised since 1808 were officered largely by well-connected men drawn from civil life. Only seventy-one West Point [the national military academy] graduates were available.[15]

The senior major general, for example, sixty-one-year-old Henry Dearborn, had fought at Bunker Hill in the 1770s and was so feeble and out of touch with military life that his men called him "Granny." And at sixty, Brigadier General William Hull, governor of the Michigan Territory, was also unfit to lead an army. Though he had served with distinction in the Revolution, he possessed no talent for leadership and had never planned a military campaign. An acquaintance described him as "a short, corpulent [fat], good-natured old gentleman who bore the marks of good eating and drinking."[16]

THE ILL-CONCEIVED STRATEGY

Still another major shortcoming of the American army in 1812 was the dubious fact that American leaders took the country into war with no overall, well-considered strategy in mind. Everyone knew that the major goal was to conquer Canada, of course. But neither the war hawks, nor the president, nor Secretary of War William Eustis, nor anyone else advanced a coordinated plan to accomplish this formidable task.

GOOD LEADERSHIP DID NOT APPEAR

In this excerpt from his massive History of the United States Army, *military historian Russell Weigley discusses the serious leadership vacuum that existed in the upper echelons of the U.S. military as the War of 1812 commenced.*

"Good leadership might . . . have accomplished something substantial in the first military project of the war, the invasion of Canada. But good leadership did not appear. James Madison had little taste or ability for the role of wartime Commander in Chief. Secretary [of War William] Eustis failed also to provide effective direction. It was typical of his performance that on the day war was declared, he ordered . . . General William Hull to hurry . . . to take command at Detroit but neglected to inform him that war had begun. Hull's consequent carelessness allowed the British to take the first trick on the Northwest frontier, the capture of a . . . schooner with the roster of Hull's forces. Similarly, for weeks Eustis allowed . . . General Henry Dearborn to command on the northern frontier without correcting Dearborn's misapprehension that his sector extended westward no farther than the Niagara. . . . To fill the highest professional ranks, Madison had to choose between young men of little or no experience or proven military skill and aged Revolutionary veterans. He chose the latter. Henry Dearborn, the former Secretary of War, and Thomas Pinckney of South Carolina, a veteran of the southern campaigns of the Revolution, received the two major generalships . . . on the eve of the war, and the roster of newly organized [generals] was completed with men who brought the average age of all general officers to sixty years."

General Henry Dearborn had previously fought in the Revolution and served as U.S. secretary of war.

Unfortunately, as it turned out, the United States ended up falling back on a contingency invasion plan that William Hull had proposed a few months before the outbreak of war, one he thought would be highly effective. In a meeting with Eustis and his aides, Hull proposed that an army be sent to the American-held Fort Detroit, located in a strategic position on the western shore of Lake Erie. The British, Hull claimed, would be intimidated by this show of force and would quickly abandon that section of Canada. When someone pointed out that the British had warships patrolling the lakes and that the United States might also need to build a lakes fleet, Hull insisted

General William Hull, who largely conceived the plan for the ill-fated expedition to Fort Detroit, as he appeared in the early 1800s.

that this would not be necessary. He assured Eustis that during their retreat the British would abandon their fleet and leave the ships conveniently in American hands.

Later, President Madison not only went along with Hull's fantastic, lamebrain scheme but also approved a plan suggested by General Dearborn. Dearborn's idea was to launch an attack along the length of Lake Champlain, in northern New York State, and strike at the Canadian city of Montreal, about fifty miles farther north. At the same time, armies from Detroit, Fort Niagara, and other points near the Great Lakes would move northward into the Montreal region. According to Hull and Dearborn, all of Canada would easily fall to the Americans in the space of a few months.

After Madison had delivered his war message on June 1, 1812, but before war was actually declared on June 18, Hull took charge of a force of some two thousand men and confidently marched them northward through the Ohio Valley toward Detroit. But his confidence faded quickly. The trail was difficult and treacherous and the forests thick and filled with swamps. Many of his men caught malaria, and some, in poor physical condition, dropped dead from exhaustion. In addition, morale declined rapidly, the soldiers increasingly fought among themselves, and worst of all, Hull seemed to lack the strength and courage needed to instill proper discipline in the troops.

Eventually, Hull and his men reached the Maumee River, which flows through northern Indiana and into Lake Erie about

The American schooner pictured here is similar in size and design to the Cuyahoga, *the boat on which William Hull loaded his heavy equipment while en route to Detroit.*

sixty miles south of Detroit. By chance, they found a small American schooner, the *Cuyahoga*, moored along the riverbank. Hull loaded his cannon and other heavy equipment into the ship and ordered the crew to sail for Detroit. Freed from carrying and dragging this equipment, he reasoned, he and his men could make better time through the wilderness. But Hull had made his first serious blunder. In addition to the heavy equipment, he had thoughtlessly placed aboard the boat a trunk containing his military plans and lists of his men and arms. Speeding down the river, the *Cuyahoga* entered Lake Erie and made for Detroit, only to be captured, along with Hull's trunk, on July 2 by the British, whose ships controlled the lakes.

ISAAC BROCK GOES ON THE OFFENSIVE

Meanwhile, British leaders in the lakes region had been considering their own strategies in preparation for the likely event of an American invasion. General George Prevost, commander of all the Canadian provinces, was worried that the British position was weak, partly because he did not have enough men to patrol and defend the entire border and also because he was unsure of where the Americans would strike first. Playing it cautious, he ordered General Isaac Brock, commander of the region surrounding Lakes Erie and Ontario, to refrain from provoking a fight, at least for the time being.

But Brock, a brilliant soldier filled with energy and determination, ignored his superior. Brock believed that it was essential to go on the offensive and attack right away to keep up the morale of his British and Indian troops. He had earlier shown his firm grasp of strategy by expanding the British lakes fleet. These ships were the key to control of the entire region because with them the British could quickly ferry men and supplies from one Canadian fort or town to another. Brock reasoned that the Americans' strongest chance for penetrating Canada would be an attack on the Niagara region between Lakes Erie and Ontario, since such a move could effectively disrupt British supply lines running from one lake to another. He did not anticipate that American leaders would fail to recognize their best opportunity, which in fact they did. So, unaware that Hull was nearing Detroit, Brock rushed his forces to the Niagara River and ordered them to prepare for an assault.

In the meantime, Hull and his bedraggled troops arrived at Fort Detroit on July 5. The fort, covering two acres, housed about eight hundred people and guarded roughly five thousand American farmers and other civilians in the area. Hull's men were itching for a fight and urged him to order an attack on nearby Fort Malden, located on the Canadian side of Lake Erie. There were few British troops defending Fort Malden at the time, and it would likely have been an easy first victory for the United States. But Hull was indecisive. He changed his mind constantly, first ordering an attack and then canceling the order, and as the days dragged on he appeared to become increasingly nervous and afraid. Having discovered that the *Cuyahoga* had been captured, along with his trunk of vital information, he feared a British attack at any moment. He also worried that Fort Detroit might soon run short of supplies. As a result, late in July, he ordered six hundred of his men to march south toward Ohio and bring back as many supplies as they could.

SURRENDER AND DISHONOR

Unfortunately for the Americans, Hull's supply detail did not get very far. The ill-fated group soon encountered Tecumseh, in command of seventy of his warriors and some forty British regulars, near the Raisin River, about fifty miles south of Detroit. Terrified and unprepared for a fight, the Americans retreated in confusion before the much smaller enemy force. Tecumseh's men proceeded to pick off the stragglers one by one while the rest of the Americans fled at top speed back to Detroit and reported the incident to the horrified William Hull.

Hull soon had even more to worry about, for on August 13 the formidable General Brock suddenly appeared on the scene. Having heard about Hull's mission several days earlier, Brock had hastily loaded his men onto a ship and sped across Lake Erie to Detroit, demonstrating the strategic value of controlling the lakes. Meeting with Tecumseh, Brock congratulated him on his victory and made him an honorary brigadier general. "A more sagacious [shrewd] or more gallant warrior does not exist," Brock said of his ally. "He was the admiration of everyone who conversed with him."[17] Tecumseh was equally impressed by the handsome and personable Brock.

Once they had gotten to know each other, the two skilled leaders got down to business. They examined the information from Hull's trunk, drew their plans, and on August 15 gave Hull a chance to avoid bloodshed. "The force at my disposal authorizes me to require the immediate surrender of Detroit,"[18] Brock told Hull in a message. When Hull did not comply, British warships sprayed the fort with cannon fire while Tecumseh's warriors surrounded the enclosure. Many of the American soldiers wanted to fight, but Hull was too frightened and upset to organize an offensive.

The next day at dawn some of those inside the fort watched in disgust as William Hull almost literally fell apart before their eyes. He sat against a wall, his voice

GENERAL HULL'S HOLLOW THREATS

On entering Canada in July 1812, General William Hull issued a proclamation (excerpted here from The Invasion of Canada *by Pierre Berton), which he was confident would (but never actually did) intimidate the locals and pave the way for an American takeover.*

"INHABITANTS OF CANADA! After thirty years of Peace and prosperity, the United States has been driven to Arms. The injuries and aggressions, the insults and indignities of Great Britain have *once more* left them no alternative but manly resistance. . . . The army under my Command has invaded your Country and the standard of the United States waves on the territory of Canada. . . . In the name of my *Country* and by the authority of my Government I promise you protection to your *persons, property, and rights.* Remain at your homes, Pursue your peaceful and customary avocations. Raise not your hands against your brethren. . . . If contrary to your own interest & the just expectation of my country, you should take part in the approaching contest, you will be considered and treated as enemies and the horrors and calamities of war will Stalk before you. If the barbarous and Savage policy of Great Britain be pursued . . . this war will be a war of extermination. The first stroke with the Tomahawk, the first attempt with the Scalping Knife will be the Signal for one indiscriminate scene of desolation. *No white man found fighting by the Side of an Indian will be taken prisoner.* Instant destruction will be his Lot."

The brilliant, resourceful Shawnee chief Tecumseh, pictured here, joined forces with Britain's General Isaac Brock for the assault on Fort Detroit.

trembling, his eyes flitting from side to side, and stuffed one wad of chewing tobacco after another into his mouth until the brown spittle dribbled out and ran down his chest. A few minutes later, he sent word to General Brock that the fort was ready to surrender.

Enraged and distraught, Hull's men reluctantly threw down their weapons, and some wept openly as British troops entered the fort. One American soldier, Private Nathaniel Adams, later wrote to his brother:

> We could have whipped hell out of the rascals but Gen. Hull has proved himself a traitor and a coward. . . .
> We were made to submit to the most

shameful surrender that ever took place in the world. Our brave Capt. Harry James cursed and swore like a pirate, and cried like his heart would break.[19]

Calling it the world's most shameful surrender was an exaggeration; but it was undoubtedly the first and only surrender of an American city to a foreign foe. William Hull's supposed master plan for the invasion of Canada had ended in unmitigated disaster and disgrace.

VICTORY AND DEFEAT ALONG THE NIAGARA

News of Detroit's fall spread swiftly around the country. Emboldened by the victory, many Indian tribes that had earlier refused to join Tecumseh's federation—the Sauk, Ottawa, Cherokee, Creek, Delaware, and others—now flocked to his side. The Great Lakes frontier in effect exploded with ambushes and massacres of American settlers, and thousands of terrified whites fled eastward. At the same time, the British moved southward into American territory and built a fort on the Raisin River. This was not only a strategically sound move but a slap in the face of American honor.

Meanwhile, the American public was calling for William Hull's head. The fall of Detroit had brought such shame and dishonor on the nation that even Thomas Jefferson, known for his understanding and forgiving nature, angrily called Hull's actions "treacherous."[20] Two years later, a military court tried Hull and sentenced him to death for cowardice in the line of duty. At the last minute, Madison pardoned him, prompting many Americans to accuse the president of being too soft.[21]

In the wake of Hull's surrender, thousands of Americans in Kentucky and Tennessee, thirsting for revenge against the British and Indians, enlisted in the army. They joined a force led by William Henry Harrison, the victor of Tippecanoe, who had replaced Hull as commander of the troops in the northwestern frontier. Late in September 1812, Harrison marched some ten thousand men northward with the intention of retaking Detroit. But heavy rains made the wilderness muddy and impassable, forcing him to put his plans on hold.

While Harrison waited, Brock acted forcefully once again. Leading sixteen hundred British troops and about three hundred Indians, he hurried back to the Niagara region, where, he had learned, the Americans had finally shown the sense to launch an attack. Soon, Brock's forces faced an American army of six thousand commanded by Stephen Van Rensselaer, a recently appointed general

The stress of battle was too much for elderly General William Hull, even though he had more soldiers than the attacking British. The American troops under his command were shocked and dismayed when he ordered them to surrender to the British.

with no previous military experience. Once again, Brock's superior military talents, combined with incompetent American leadership, spelled disaster for the United States. Van Rensselaer unwisely divided his forces, and Brock's regulars and Indians cut most of a group of eight hundred Americans to pieces while the rest of the American army stood idly by only a few miles away.

In a sense, however, the battle ended up being both a victory and a defeat for the British. Though they had triumphed and further disgraced the Americans, during the fighting Isaac Brock had taken a shot in the chest and perished. Never again would the British in Canada have a commander of his enormous gifts and stature, and his death greatly decreased the chances for a British victory in a prolonged land war.

AN INGLORIOUS CHAPTER FOR THE UNITED STATES

For the moment, however, American embarrassments and defeats continued. Planning to invade Canada, General Alexander Smythe led a force of six thousand U.S. troops to the Niagara River in November 1812. The soldiers boarded boats and were less than halfway across when Smythe ordered a retreat and, without offering an explanation, simply called off the expedition. According to

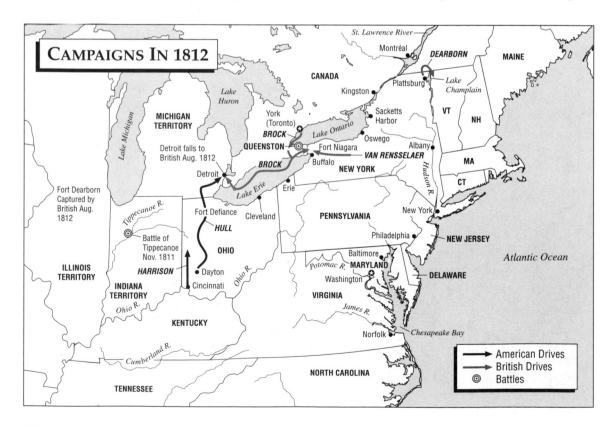

THE RELIABLE AND DEADLY MUSKET

The musket, or flintlock, is a primitive rifle that was used extensively by the world's armies from the 1500s to the 1800s. One loaded a musket by pouring gunpowder down the front barrel, then inserting a lead ball. Pulling the trigger released a metal hammer that struck a piece of flint, which in turn produced a spark that ignited the powder. The explosion then pushed the ball out of the barrel. Muskets could fire up to two hundred yards, but it took from thirty seconds to a minute to load one, and they were not very accurate. Nevertheless, except for cannon, they were the most reliable and deadly weapons available.

A major advance in musket design occurred in 1801, just prior to the War of 1812, when the U.S. government hired inventor Eli Whitney to produce thousands of muskets for the American army. This was a tremendously difficult and expensive task at the time. For centuries, people had made the weapons by hand, taking up to a week to make just one, and no two muskets were exactly alike. To mass-produce the rifles, Whitney had to create many new machines and other labor-saving devices.

With a government advance of only $5,000, he set up a factory in New Haven, Connecticut, a plant that later became a model for American industry. His most ingenious idea was to use identical and interchangeable parts, making each weapon the same. Whitney invited a group of congressmen and other notables, including Thomas Jefferson, to gather around a table covered with dozens of assorted musket parts. He challenged them to put the pieces together, then load and fire. They easily completed the task and were so impressed that they gave Whitney three times the money he had asked for to continue developing the idea.

The musket was used by armies for over three centuries. In 1801, Eli Whitney made the musket even more easy to use for large numbers of troops when he invented interchangeable parts for the weapon.

some witnesses, his men were so upset that they shot him, taking care to make it look like an accident.

General Dearborn's long heralded attempt to cross Lake Champlain and capture Montreal fared no better. His force of seven thousand men engaged about nineteen hundred British Canadians north of the lake on the evening of November 19. After an initial skirmish, most of the Americans got lost and began firing on one another, after which they informed Dearborn that they would go no farther. Mortified, Dearborn had no choice but to cancel the rest of the campaign.

The Americans' grand conquest of Canada had turned out to be a sad demonstration of their lack of military preparedness and leadership. As noted historian Robert Leckie aptly phrases it, the campaign was "the most inglorious chapter in American military history."[22] By early 1813, thousands of American settlers and soldiers had died, Britain had retained control of the Great Lakes, U.S. forces had become a laughingstock, and the frontier was more dangerous than ever. Many in Congress blamed Madison, saying that he should have appointed better, more experienced officers. They also faulted him for not building a lakes fleet, which they finally saw was vital to gaining control of the region.

As the president worked to correct these mistakes, he reminded his critics that all was not lost. And indeed, during the same months that the frontier campaigns had bogged down in mud and disgrace, miles to the east American warships had unexpectedly and heroically turned defeat into victory and emerged as the pride of the nation.

3 Victories on the Open Sea

When the United States declared war on Great Britain in June 1812, American leaders planned to use the vessels of the small U.S. war fleet mainly to defend the Atlantic coast. They also hoped these ships might capture or destroy some of the British cargo ships carrying supplies bound for Canada. Challenging British warships for mastery of the Atlantic seemed out of the question, since the Royal Navy was by far the world's largest and no one on either side believed for a second that the U.S. stood a chance on the open seas.

Indeed, Britain's naval power in 1812 was immense. It had more than 600 warships, including some 120 ships of the line (each of which, carrying between fifty and eighty or more cannon, was an early version of a modern battleship). The Royal Navy also featured between 115 and 120 frigates, smaller and faster than ships of the line and able to carry between thirty-two and forty-four big guns. These vessels were commanded by superb officers and usually manned with well-trained, experienced crews. By contrast, the late noted naval historian Dudley Knox writes, the U.S. Navy

had no ships-of-the-line; and excluding condemned ships, only three 44-gun frigates, three 38-gun frigates, three sloops-of-war [small, single-masted ships] mounting 32, 28, and 18 guns respectively, besides seven smaller vessels ranging down to 12 guns each.[23]

Considering this enormous disparity in numbers and firepower of the two navies, no one at the time doubted that the Americans were hopelessly outclassed. Although the bulk of Britain's naval forces was engaged in the European war, the several dozen warships committed to American waters appeared to be more than enough to deal with the tiny U.S. fleet. With complete confidence, British naval officers looked with contempt on their "inferior" American counterparts.

SOME BRASH YOUNG U.S. OFFICERS

Perhaps the only significant advantage the U.S. Navy possessed at the time was that its senior officers were mostly young, brash, and eager to show the arrogant British captains what American sailors

Isaac Hull was one of a few key naval commanders who managed to disprove the common notion that the British navy was unbeatable.

Hamilton's caution about engaging the enemy only when absolutely necessary was part of an American strategy designed to save as many ships as possible to defend the coastal cities. But Hull and his fellow captains had no intention of waiting for the British to come to them. For years American seamen had endured insult after insult by British ships, and U.S. captains felt that it was now time to even the score.

During the last days of June, Hull carefully prepared his ship for departure. He was nothing like his uncle, the inept William Hull, who was at that moment marching his troops on their ill-fated trek to Detroit. The younger Hull, a talented, experienced seaman, methodically scrutinized every supply list and crate during the loading of the forty-four-gun *Constitution*. Most of the sailors in his 450-man crew were new recruits who had never been on a large warship, so he trained and drilled them almost day and night. (The crew included several marines who were expert shots with muskets, which would be used if they came close enough to an enemy ship.) At noon on July 4, the *Constitution* fired a fifteen-gun salute in honor of the nation's thirty-sixth birthday; the next day it sailed from Annapolis, Maryland, for an unexpected date with destiny.

were made of. Only a few hours after the American war declaration on June 18, 1812, one of these American officers, thirty-five-year-old Isaac Hull, captain of the frigate *Constitution*, received his orders from Navy Secretary Paul Hamilton. War had been declared, Hamilton wrote,

> and you are with the force under your command entitled to every belligerent right to attack and capture, and to defend—You will use the utmost dispatch to reach New York. . . . You will not fail to notice the British flag, should it present itself—I am informed that the [British warship] *Belvidera* is on our coast, but you are not to understand me as impelling you to battle . . . unless attacked, or with a reasonable prospect of success, of which you are to be . . . the judge.[24]

THE "GREAT CHASE"

One of history's most famous and exciting naval encounters began at about 2:00 P.M. on July 16, 1812, when Hull's lookout sighted several sails on the horizon. At

OLD IRONSIDES

The USS *Constitution* is the most famous ship in the history of the U.S. Navy. Designed by Joshua Humphreys and built in Boston between 1794 and 1797, it was one of the navy's first three war frigates. It was constructed of live oak, red cedar, and hard pine, had a length of 204 feet, and weighed 2,200 tons. Famed patriot and silversmith Paul Revere crafted the copper sheathing on the ship's bottom. The vessel's design called for forty-four cannon with ranges of up to 1,200 yards each, and it carried a crew of 450 sailors and marines. The total cost of the *Constitution* in 1797 was $302,718.

After seeing action against the French (1797–1798) and against North African pirates (1801–1805), the ship earned eternal glory for its exploits in the War of 1812. In addition to defeating the *Guerriere,* the *Constitution* successfully outran five British warships and sank several others. By 1828, the navy was about to dismantle the aging Old Ironsides, but public sentiment saved the vessel and it was carefully restored. In the 1900s, it sailed to more than a hundred U.S. ports, where millions of people toured it. Permanently docked in Boston, it remains a commissioned ship in the U.S. fleet.

The USS Constitution, *shown here on one of its annual turnaround cruises, is still a fully commissioned ship in the U.S. fleet.*

such a distance, there was no way to tell whether they were friend or foe, so Hull steered directly for the vessels in an attempt to identify them. By 5:00 the next morning, there was no longer any doubt: Five British warships were closing in at top speed on the American vessel. There were four frigates—the *Shannon*, *Belvidera*, *Aeolus*, and *Guerriere*—along with the sixty-four-gun ship of the line *Africa*. Hull believed that the *Constitution* was a match for any ship in single combat, but he realized that facing five ships was plain suicide. Since he could not risk allowing the United States to lose one of its best warships, there was no choice but to make a run for it.

Hull decided that if he had to retreat, he would do so fighting. He had part of the stern (back) rail cut away from the ship and mounted one of his biggest cannon there, facing the rear. He also ordered some sailors to widen the portholes in his rear-facing cabin and to poke cannon through these openings; and (as he later recalled) he "cleared the ship for action, being determined they should not get her without resistance on our part."[25]

Less than an hour after the *Constitution* had turned to flee, the wind suddenly died down, leaving the American frigate dead in the water with the enemy squadron closing in just twelve miles away. Without hesitation, Hull ordered some of the cutters (or "long boats," large rowboats) lowered. After attaching ropes to the ship's front, sailors in the cutters began to row with all their might, attempting to drag the ship forward. A few minutes later, Hull observed the enemy ships through his telescope. Sure enough, the *Belvidera* and *Shannon* had also lowered their cutters to try to tow the ships clear of the calm sea.

By 7:00 A.M., it was obvious that the British, with more cutters in the water, were quickly gaining on the American ship. In desperation, Hull now ordered his men to start kedging, a process explained here by one of the *Constitution*'s modern-day skippers:

> Kedging involves using long boats to carry an anchor ahead of the ship, dropping it, and then, by means of the ship's anchor capstan [device for lifting the anchor], hauling the ship up to a position over the anchor. While this is being done, a second anchor is taken out and dropped, to repeat the process as the original anchor is . . . again taken forward by a ship's boat. By stages, a sailing ship could be moved in a given direction despite . . . the absence of a wind.[26]

At 7:30, with the *Belvidera* closing in to less than half a mile, Hull hoisted the American flag and ordered the rear cannon to open fire. Although the shot fell short, the British rowers became wary and temporarily slowed down. However, the *Shannon* pressed onward and the *Guerriere* swung wide to attack the *Constitution* from the side, while the huge battleship *Africa* loomed ever closer. Soon, the British transferred cutters from the *Aeolus* to the *Belvidera* and *Shannon*, and the extra rowers further increased the speed of the two lead pursuers.

By 9:00, the *Belvidera* was within firing distance, and its bow (front) cannon

The Constitution *escapes from the British squadron after a chase lasting almost sixty hours.*

blazed. As the shots skimmed the water just short of the *Constitution*'s stern, the American sailors let loose a loud shout of defiance. The American frigate's guns answered with a roar, one cannonball smashing into the *Belvidera*'s main deck. Next, the *Guerriere* opened fire, but its shots, like those of its sister ship, fell short.

COURAGE, ENDURANCE, AND TEAMWORK

The grueling process of towing and kedging dragged on until 11:00 A.M., when a breeze finally blew up. Hull ordered extra sail raised, and the *Constitution* suddenly sped forward, overtaking its own cutters. But the British now had the advantage of the wind as well, and the chase continued at full throttle into the afternoon, when Hull ordered most of the drinking water—twenty-three hundred gallons of it—thrown overboard to lighten the ship. This helped, and the gap between the *Constitution* and its pursuers widened from half a mile to nearly two miles.

Later that day and all through the night, the wind periodically appeared and disappeared. And hour after hour, exhausted men from both navies rowed until their muscles cramped, many catching short naps as they sat upright in the tiny cutters. Isaac Hull refused to leave his command post on the deck to take a rest and occasionally even helped his men turn the backbreaking capstan.

At dawn, Hull saw that the tireless efforts of his crew had maintained the ship's two-mile lead. An hour later the wind increased, and the *Constitution* gained a burst of speed. The *Guerriere* and *Aeolus* now attempted to sail landward to cut off the Americans' escape route to the coast; but the *Constitution*'s speed and some clever maneuvering by Hull foiled that plan, and the gap between the Americans and British continued to widen. The chase continued well into the afternoon of July 19, at which point Hull could make out only one of the enemy warships trailing far behind. Finally, the British, angry and exhausted, and in Hull's words, "finding that they were fast dropping astern, gave over chase [i.e., called it quits], and hauled their wind to the northward, probably for . . . New York."[27]

The ship was now safe. In a gesture of respect the entire crew of the *Constitution* stood at silent attention as Hull, who had not slept a wink in more than three days, made his way toward his cabin. As he was about to go below, a crewman thanked him for his courage and dedication. In the days and weeks that followed, other members of his crew did the same, and he was acclaimed as a hero. Hull's response was to show both modesty and loyalty to his crew by issuing a public notice saying that most of the credit belonged to the "brave officers and the crew . . . for their very great exertions and prompt attention to orders while the enemy were in chase."[28] In truth, the incredible feat had been accomplished by inspired teamwork. As naval historian Tyrone Martin puts it,

> Isaac Hull and his crew, who had been together at sea for just . . . [a few]

days, had outsailed a numerically superior British squadron in a 57-hour demonstration of endurance, teamwork, and skilled seamanship. It would not be the last time that this combination would embarrass their English cousins.[29]

A BRITISH CAPTAIN'S CHALLENGE

The *Constitution*'s successful evasion of the British squadron seemed to prove what American officers had been saying for a long time—namely, that they and their crews were just as skilled as their British counterparts. Encouraged and emboldened by Hull's demonstration, American warships now stepped up their attacks on British shipping. The U.S. frigates *President*, *United States*, and *Congress*, as well as smaller warships like the *Hornet* and *Argus*, intercepted many British cargo ships attempting to get through to Canada.

But the British remained unimpressed by the "Yankee upstarts" who dared to challenge their mastery of the sea. Captain James Dacres, of the *Guerriere*, publicly scoffed at the American navy. He said that the escape of the *Constitution* was nothing but a lucky break and issued an open challenge to any American ship to come out and fight him. His vessel, he boasted, would quickly send any U.S. frigate to the bottom of the sea.

Isaac Hull, overseeing the *Constitution*'s resupplying in Boston, was eager to answer Dacres's challenge. Hull sailed on August 2, 1812, and managed to capture three British cargo ships in the following two weeks. All the while, he searched for the *Guerriere*, which he knew was somewhere in the area. At about 2:00 P.M. on August 19, the American lookout sighted a sail several miles to the south. As the ships neared each other, Hull and his officers tensed with excite-

ment, for the British frigate bearing down on them was none other than the *Guerriere*. Captain Dacres recognized the *Constitution* and informed his crew that the American ship could not be allowed to escape this time.

Both captains immediately tried to position their ships for the "weather gauge,"

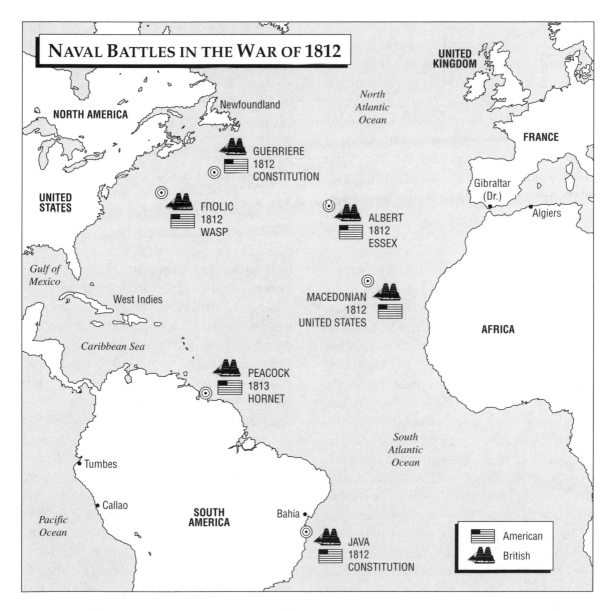

NAVAL BATTLES IN THE WAR OF 1812

UNITED KINGDOM

NORTH AMERICA

Newfoundland

North Atlantic Ocean

FRANCE

UNITED STATES

GUERRIERE 1812 CONSTITUTION

Gibraltar (Br.)

Algiers

FROLIC 1812 WASP

ALBERT 1812 ESSEX

Gulf of Mexico

West Indies

MACEDONIAN 1812 UNITED STATES

AFRICA

Caribbean Sea

PEACOCK 1813 HORNET

South Atlantic Ocean

Tumbes

Callao

SOUTH AMERICA

Bahia

Pacific Ocean

JAVA 1812 CONSTITUTION

American

British

a strategic position attained by moving behind the enemy vessel while keeping one's own sails in the wind. A ship that gained this advantage could turn sideways and fire its cannon at the enemy's undefended stern. For forty-five minutes, Hull and Dacres flitted and danced around each other, each displaying amazing skill but neither able to outmaneuver the other. At one point, Dacres fired the cannon on his port (left) side, but the shots fell short. A few minutes later he tried again, and this time the cannonballs whizzed over the *Constitution*'s masts.

In the meantime, Hull had spun his own ship around. In a sudden surprise maneuver, he sailed directly toward the front of the British frigate, his intention being to veer off at the last moment and fire his cannon "broadsides" as he moved by the other ship. As the *Constitution* closed in, the American sailors repeatedly begged Hull to allow them to shoot. But each time he ordered them to wait. Realizing his predicament, Dacres tried desperately to pull away. But it was too late, for seconds later the *Constitution* closed in to within fifty feet, and Hull screamed, "Now boys, pour it into them!"[30] As the American gunners opened fire with a vengeance, blast after blast pounded the *Guerriere*, tearing rigging and sails to pieces. The British gunners tried to return fire, but most of their shots missed, and the ones that found their mark had little effect. According to both American and British eyewitnesses, several British cannonballs simply bounced harmlessly off the *Constitution*'s hard wooden hull. "Her sides are made of iron!"[31] an American

sailor exclaimed, giving birth to the nickname the vessel proudly bears to this day—"Old Ironsides."

THE *GUERRIERE*'S END

The *Constitution* continued to blast away at Dacres's nearly defenseless ship. Then the wind suddenly shifted and the frigates drifted dangerously close to each other. Before either captain could pull away, the *Guerriere*'s bowsprit (front-pointing mast) became tangled in the *Constitution*'s rigging, locking the ships in a deadly embrace. Seconds later, boarding parties from both vessels surged forward. The American assault was led by Lieutenant Charles Morris, who received a shot directly in the face, and Lieutenant William Bush, whose stomach was torn open by musket fire. While the ships heaved up and down in the rolling sea, sailors armed with swords slashed at each other until streams of blood flowed across the decks. Hull was about to order a second boarding party to attack when the ships suddenly untangled and lurched apart, the violent movement causing the British ship's foremast and main mast to topple down.

Less than two hours after the fight had begun, Captain Dacres, now wounded and humbled, surrendered. The *Guerriere*, a helpless wreck, listed in the water. Its losses were twenty-three dead and fifty-six wounded, while the Americans had sustained seven dead and seven wounded. The next day, after transferring the British survivors to his own ship, Hull ordered

The Constitution, *nicknamed "Old Ironsides," seemed invincible. By the end of the War of 1812, the* Constitution *had successfully outrun five British warships and had sunk several others.*

the enemy vessel blown up and stood silently beside Dacres while the *Guerriere* met its end at 3:15 P.M., August 20, 1812. According to one of Hull's officers,

> There was something melancholy and grand in the sight. Although the frigate was a wreck . . . she bore marks of her former greatness. . . . Her long, high, black sides rose in solitary majesty before us as we bade her farewell. . . . She was about to sink into the deep ocean forever. . . . Scarcely a word was spoken on board the *Constitution*, so breathless was the interest felt in the scene. . . . There was a . . . shuddering motion, and streams of light, like streaks of lightning running along the sides; and the grand

crash came! The quarterdeck . . . lifted like a mass, broke into fragments, and flew in every direction. The hull, parted in the center by the shock . . . reeled, staggered, plunged forward a few feet, and sank out of sight. It was a grand and awful scene.[32]

IN LONDON, SHOCK AND BEWILDERMENT

In their victory, the first time that an American warship had ever defeated a British one, Hull and his crew had shattered the myth of the British navy's invincibility. One American politician commented that the battle had instantly raised the United States to the rank of a first-class naval

CAPTAIN DACRES PERFORMS A SAD DUTY

This excerpt (quoted in volume 1 of Dudley's Naval War of 1812*) is from the letter dispatched on September 7, 1812, by British sea captain James Dacres to his superior, officially informing him that the* Guerriere *had been lost. Note how Dacres honorably and graciously gives due credit to his adversary.*

"Sir, I am sorry to inform you of the Capture of His Majesty's late Ship *Guerriere* by the American Frigate *Constitution* after a severe action on the 19th of August. . . . [He gives a lengthy description of the fight.] The *Guerriere* was so cut up, that all attempts to get her in would have been useless. As soon as the wounded were got out of her, they set her on fire, and I feel it my duty to state that the conduct of Captain Hull and his Officers to our Men has been that of a brave Enemy, the greatest care being taken to prevent our Men losing the smallest trifle, and the greatest attention being paid to the wounded who . . . I hope will do well. . . . I hope, in considering the circumstances, you will think the Ship entrusted to my charge was properly defended. . . . The Enemy had such an advantage from his Marines and Riflemen, when close, and his superior sailing enabled him to choose his distance. I enclose herewith a List of killed and wounded on board the *Guerriere*."

The battle between the American ship Constitution *and the British ship* Guerriere *(in foreground) ended in a dramatic victory for the Americans.*

In this nineteenth-century painting (left), the American warship United States, *piloted by Commander Stephen Decatur (below), seizes the British frigate* Macedonian *after crippling it in battle.*

power (an exaggeration, but an understandable one given the euphoria of the moment). There were celebrations in every American city, and Hull was once again hailed as a hero.

By contrast, the British were shocked and bewildered. The London *Times* reported, "The Loss of the *Guerriere* spreads a degree of gloom through the town which it was painful to observe."[33] Later, the newspaper stated that the British ship had fallen to "a new enemy, an enemy unaccustomed to such triumphs and likely to be rendered insolent and confident by them." Above all, the *Times* emphasized, "there is one object to which our most strenuous efforts should be directed—the entire annihilation of the American Navy."[34]

American captains were indeed "rendered more confident" by Hull's triumph and quickly scored more victories on the open sea. On October 18, the USS *Wasp* defeated the British *Frolic*; on October 25, the *Constitution*'s sister ship, the *United States*, commanded by Stephen Decatur, mangled the frigate *Macedonian*; and in December, Hull's ship won another battle, this time destroying the frigate *Java*. Not surprisingly, the British viewed this string of American wins with horror and disbe-lief. In late December, the *Times* asked in dismay, "What is wrong with British sea power?"[35]

The American victories taught both sides important lessons. British naval officers grudgingly began to respect their American cousins and to be less overconfident in engaging them. At the same time, James Madison and other U.S. leaders recognized their own navy's potential and took steps

The British frigate Java *is destroyed by a fiery explosion after doing battle with the USS* Constitution *in December 1812.*

Common Mishaps Aboard Ship

This excerpt from an August 1812 entry in the journal of the Constitution's *surgeon, Amos Evans, illustrates some of the common and serious hazards that the wooden warships of the time risked even when they were not engaged in battle (quoted in Tyrone Martin's* A Most Fortunate Ship).

"Were alarmed about 9 o'clock with the cry of fire in the cockpit—produced by one of the Surgeon's mates having left a candle burning in his state room. . . . The cry of fire is dreadful on shore, but ten thousand times more distressing on board a powder ship at sea. It produced much confusion but was instantly extinguished. The Surgeon's mate, who is truly a worthy fellow, was arrested for his negligence. . . . At 3 P.M. a sailor (John Lindsy) fell overboard out of the main chains. The topsail was instantly backed and the stern boat lowered down. The man being (fortunately) an expert swimmer, kept on top of the water, and was picked up about 200 yards astern. He said he could have taken off his shoes, but did not wish to lose them! The blood however appeared to have forsaken his cheeks. The tenure of a sailor's existence is certainly more precarious than any other man's, a soldier's not excepted. Who would not be a sailor? I, for one."

to expand it as rapidly as possible. For the moment, the Atlantic fleet appeared able to hold its own; the more pressing need for new ships was in the Great Lakes region, where the United States still had no fleet at all. It was painfully clear that even if U.S. ships continued to do well in the open ocean, as long as the British controlled the lakes, the Americans had no hope of winning the war.

4 Battle for the Great Lakes

The lack of warships and supply vessels on Lakes Erie and Ontario put the United States at a severe disadvantage in the first year of the War of 1812. During the disastrous Canadian campaign, Isaac Brock, the British commander who captured Detroit, showed the importance of controlling the region by using the vast system of connected lakes and rivers to move troops quickly from one place to another. He also used these waterways to ferry a constant stream of weapons and other commodities from the Atlantic coast. A steady supply of food was essential, for thousands of British soldiers and their Indian allies had to be fed, and the undeveloped wilderness surrounding the Great Lakes provided little grain and few cattle. On all counts, then, there was simply no way to sustain large armies in the region without mastery of the lakes.

The necessity of controlling the lakes became clear to the Americans once again during the winter of 1812–1813, a few months after William Henry Harrison had halted his army south of Lake Erie because of mud from heavy rains. Harrison's men were hungry and lacked supplies, including proper winter clothing. In January 1813, he ordered them to break camp and march north, hoping to retake Detroit. Harrison sent twelve hundred of his men, under the command of General James Winchester, up ahead to establish a base camp near the lake. On January 22, Winchester's force was surprised near the Raisin River by a force of British and Indians led by Colonel Henry Proctor, Brock's successor. Thanks to the British lakes fleet, Proctor was well supplied and his men were well fed. British ships helped move many of his troops within striking distance of the Americans; he attacked, and after the Americans surrendered, the Indians massacred the survivors. The lack of supplies and the winter cold then took their toll on the rest of Harrison's army. His expedition ended in failure a few weeks later, largely because the British controlled the lakes and the major supply lines intersecting them.

ENTER ISAAC CHAUNCEY AND OLIVER PERRY

Even before the onset of Harrison's misfortunes, President Madison had become determined to eliminate the British lakes fleet and gain control of the northwestern frontier. He put Commodore Isaac Chauncey, of the New York Navy Yard, in charge of creating and commanding an American fleet on Lakes Erie and Ontario. Late in 1812, Chauncey began establishing supply bases near the eastern shores of the lakes and had several small lake craft transported overland to the bases. There, the craft were refitted and converted into fighting vessels. He also brought green timber, miles of cord, cartloads of canvas, and dozens of cannon, hoping to build several more ships, including at least two small frigates. Used to ocean vessels, Chauncey faced the task of adapting this

knowledge to what John Elting calls the "peculiarities" of lake warfare. "Ontario was deep water," Elting explains,

capable of taking large vessels, but because of ice was navigable for roughly only half the year. Lake merchant vessels therefore usually were lightly built schooners with large spreads of sail for swift, good-weather cruising. When armed as improvised warships, their guns made them top-heavy and tricky to handle. A ship built specifically as a warship for lake service could have more

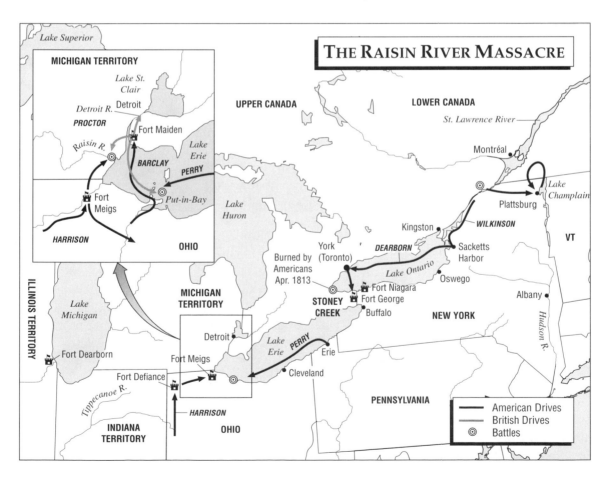

cannon than a sea-going vessel of the same size, since it did not have to carry either fresh water for its crew or large quantities of food and other supplies. But such ships, whether British or American, would have to be hastily constructed from green timber, at the end of long and sometimes impossible supply lines.[36]

What Chauncey lacked most was the right man to train the crews and oversee the building of the new ships. In this regard he was in luck, for in the last weeks of 1812 a twenty-eight-year-old naval officer, Oliver Hazard Perry, wrote to him and offered his services. Having first gone to sea at the age of eleven, Perry was a gifted sailor and effective leader. De-

MASSACRE ON THE RAISIN RIVER

Here, from his informative study of the War of 1812, former Ohio State University scholar Harry L. Coles describes what happened to General James Winchester and his men after General Harrison sent them to establish a base camp near Detroit in preparation for an assault on that town.

"Though snow fell to a depth of two feet, Winchester's force . . . reached the rapids [of the Maumee River] on January 10 [1813] and began to lay out a fortified camp. . . . As soon as he heard the news of the American advance, Colonel [Henry] Proctor [the British commander in the region] realized that the Americans had overextended themselves. On January 21, with from 1,200 to 1,400 men [about half of them Indians], he crossed the river on the ice. . . . Outnumbered and without artillery, Winchester should have deployed his men so that the Raisin River was to his front instead of his rear. . . . [His mistake] enabled Proctor, when he attacked about four o'clock on the twenty-first, to overwhelm quickly the American right. . . . Winchester tried in vain to rally his men. Before anything could be done, however, the Indians got to the rear and literally hacked the Americans to pieces. At least one hundred Kentuckians were scalped within a few minutes. The rest were captured, including General Winchester. . . . [After Proctor and his British regulars] left, the Indians . . . hunted down the [American] wounded and scalped them. Coming across one house with several prisoners, they set it afire and as the wounded tried to escape . . . the Indians beat them back with tomahawks. . . . 'Remember the River Raisin' soon became the rallying cry of the soldiers of the Northwestern Army."

Oliver Hazard Perry is credited with creating the U.S. fleet that took control of Lake Erie on September 10, 1813. It was his leadership and determination that led to the successful defense of the Great Lakes.

lighted, Chauncey wrote back to Perry, "You are just the man I have been looking for,"[37] and immediately recommended Perry for the job to Navy Secretary William Jones.

Perry arrived at Presque Isle, the future site of the city of Erie, located on the lake's southern shore, in March 1813 and took over the American shipbuilding operation. By April, six ships were under construction—two twenty-gun vessels and four smaller gunboats with two to four cannon each. Perry realized that these six vessels were not nearly enough to defeat the British, and he itched to get his hands on five of Chauncey's ships that were presently docked at Black Rock, on the Niagara River between Lakes Erie and Ontario. The problem was that the British

fleet, under the command of Captain Robert Barclay, had the area blockaded so that Chauncey's ships were trapped.

BRITISH PROBLEMS AND STRATEGIES

Though possessing the advantage, Barclay too faced some serious problems. He had only five ships—the *Lady Charlotte*, with eighteen guns; the *Lady Prevost*, with twelve guns; and three smaller gunboats—while the twenty-gun *Detroit* was under construction at Fort Malden. This small fleet had been more than ample to control Lake Erie when the Americans had no fleet of their own. But soon, Barclay realized, Perry's ships would be completed. And if Perry's group could link up with Chauncey's ships at Black Rock, the British would be badly outnumbered and outgunned. Barclay also faced increasing supply and manpower problems. Most of the supplies that came from the East went to the British and Indian land troops, and his sailors had to make do with what was left. Even worse, he did not have enough men and cannon to outfit his new warship, the *Detroit*, in an adequate manner.

Barclay's situation seemed to worsen in late May 1813 when American troops moved into the Niagara region, forcing him to lift his blockade against Black Rock. The five U.S. ships stationed there were now free for service, and Perry promptly sent officers to sail them to Presque Isle. At the same time, General Harrison arrived in the Lake Erie region at the head of another army. When Harrison did

TRAVELING THE GREAT LAKES SYSTEM

In the 1700s and early 1800s, the term *Great Lakes* referred mainly to Lakes Erie and Ontario, and included the numerous rivers that flow from and into them. These lakes and rivers form a huge system of interconnected waterways that stretch from Detroit, on the western shore of Lake Erie, all the way to the Atlantic Ocean. Most of the original Canadian forts and towns, including Detroit, Toronto, Montreal, and Quebec, were clustered along these waterways, on which the British were able to transport troops and supplies into Canada and the American frontier almost completely over water.

To reach Detroit from the Atlantic in 1812, travelers sailed their ship into the Gulf of St. Lawrence, north of Nova Scotia. This two-hundred-mile-wide bay leads to the St. Lawrence River, which stretches southwestward for some 760 miles. At the head of the St. Lawrence, the ship entered Lake Ontario, which averages 800 feet in depth and covers more than 7,500 square miles. After sailing more than 150 miles across the lake, the vessel entered the Niagara River. At Niagara Falls, where the land rises nearly 200 feet, the travelers crossed overland to another ship anchored upriver from the falls. The second vessel continued along the river to Lake Erie, about 210 feet deep, with an area of over 9,900 square miles. After a journey of about 200 miles across the lake, the travelers finally reached Detroit.

The magnificent cascading waters of Niagara Falls mark the point where the land between Lakes Erie and Ontario rises almost 200 feet.

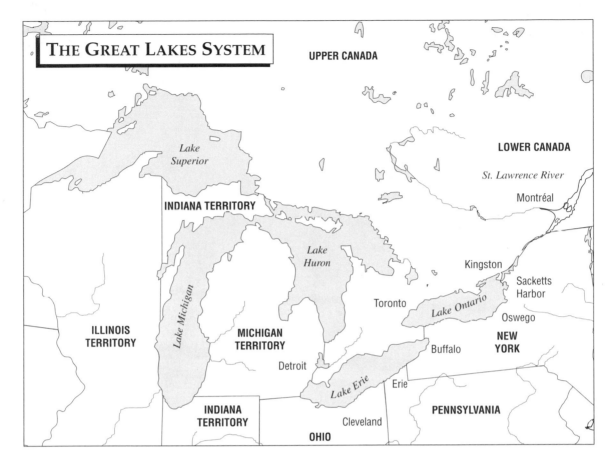

THE GREAT LAKES SYSTEM

UPPER CANADA

LOWER CANADA

St. Lawrence River

Montréal

Lake Superior

INDIANA TERRITORY

Lake Huron

Kingston

Sacketts Harbor

Toronto

Lake Ontario

Oswego

Lake Michigan

ILLINOIS TERRITORY

MICHIGAN TERRITORY

NEW YORK

Buffalo

Detroit

Lake Erie

Erie

INDIANA TERRITORY

PENNSYLVANIA

Cleveland

OHIO

not immediately move on Fort Malden, Barclay realized that the American general was waiting for Perry to complete the U.S. fleet and engage the British.

Barclay decided that his best chance to defeat Perry was to take the British fleet to Presque Isle and try to destroy the American fleet before it was completed. When Barclay approached the American base in June, however, he found the harbor blocked by a wide, submerged sandbar. Unable to get his ships close enough to fire on the Americans, he anchored his fleet and blockaded the harbor.

At this juncture, Barclay's next best plan would have been a land attack on the American base; however, he barely had enough sailors to man his ships, plus Perry's position was too well defended. So Barclay decided that the smartest thing to do was wait. He knew that the only way Perry could get his own newly built ships out onto the lake was to drag them across the bar. During such an operation, the vessels would be exposed and helpless, and Barclay would easily be able to move in and destroy them. Surely, the British captain reasoned, his opponent would have the sense to stay put on the landward side of the bar, leaving Barclay in control of the lake.

British officers, seamen, and marines from the British frigate Shannon
board the Chesapeake *and haul down the Stars and Stripes.*

PERRY CROSSES THE BAR

On July 12, 1813, as his ships neared completion, Oliver Perry received distressing news. The British frigate *Shannon* had defeated the American frigate *Chesapeake* off the coast of Massachusetts in early June. The *Chesapeake*'s commander, Captain James Lawrence, whom Perry greatly admired, had perished in the battle, leaving behind the dying words, "Don't give up the ship! Fight her till she sinks!"[38] Moved and inspired, Perry had a blue flag made, one similar in style to Lawrence's own banner, and ordered that the message

"Don't give up the ship" be sewn into it. Perry hoisted the flag above his new flagship, which he officially christened the *Lawrence* in honor of his martyred fellow captain. He named his other new twenty-gun vessel the *Niagara.*

A few days later, Perry received orders from Chauncey to sail out onto the lake and attack the British. But Perry faced two major difficulties. First, he did not have enough men to operate his ships properly, and second, Barclay's vessels still guarded the waters beyond the sandbar. How could Perry be expected to launch an attack under these conditions?

He wrote to Chauncey, begging, "For God's sake, and yours and mine, send me men."[39] Chauncey could spare only sixty men, mostly sick or inexperienced, and the frustrated Perry fired back to his superior, "The men that came are a motley set. . . . I cannot think you saw them after they were selected—I am however pleased to see anything in the shape of a man."[40] Still desperate for more men, Perry combed the countryside, offering any farmers and woodsmen he could find $10 each to serve on his ships for four months. But by the last day of July, he had managed to scrape together only three hundred men, far fewer than he needed. Making matters worse, at this same moment he learned that Barclay had just launched the *Detroit*, armed with twenty cannon.

Captain James Lawrence is mortally wounded on the Chesapeake *during the fight with the British. Lawrence's dying words, "Don't Give Up the Ship," greatly inspired Oliver Perry and other American captains.*

Then, quite suddenly, the situation changed in Perry's favor. On August 1, 1813, the Americans awoke to find that Barclay's fleet had left during the night. Perry was dumbfounded and could only conclude that his adversary had departed to aid some British fort under American attack. But in reality, the British withdrawal was the result of a combination of supply problems and poor planning; specifically, Barclay had not brought sufficient provisions for a lengthy blockade and finally had no choice but to withdraw to Fort Malden, a strategic blunder that would soon cost the British dearly.

Perry wasted no time in taking advantage of the situation. He ordered every able-bodied person in the area to help get his ships over the sandbar. They first towed the vessels out into the harbor until they were near the bar, which lay about four feet beneath the surface. Then gangs of sailors brought in "camels," large hollow floats topped by decks of wood. The workers filled the floats with water so that they sank down beneath the level of the ships' portholes; then they ran long timbers through the portholes, allowing the ends of the timbers to rest on the decks of the camels. Next, the sailors drained the water from the camels, which rose, in the process carrying the ships upward. As the vessels floated high in the water, teams of sailors rowing cutters dragged them over the bar. Working day and night, Perry's teams managed to get all the ships out

In the Battle of Lake Erie, fought on September 10, 1813, Perry's flagship, the USS Lawrence (listing at center), comes under ferocious attack by several British ships.

Having temporarily vacated his crippled flagship, Perry, cradling its flag, desperately heads for the Niagara, *hoping to turn the tide of the battle.*

onto the lake by August 5, by which time Barclay was on his way back to resume the blockade. But it was too late. Seeing the new American fleet fully deployed, Barclay dared not attack and returned in frustration to Fort Malden.

THE BATTLE OF LAKE ERIE

Now enjoying almost complete freedom to roam Lake Erie, Perry quickly established another base at Put-in-Bay, on the western shore of the lake, just south of Fort Malden. On August 10, Chauncey sent him ninety more sailors, led by young Lieutenant Jesse Elliott, whom

Perry immediately placed in command of the *Niagara*. A few days later, General Harrison, whose forces were camped south of the lake, sent Perry about a hundred Kentucky sharpshooters, dressed in buckskins and carrying muskets. Although these men had never served on a ship, Perry was an excellent teacher and gave them a thorough primer in the basics of seamanship.

With his ships afloat and his crews trained, Perry was eager to engage the enemy. He got his chance on September 10, 1813. All through August, General Proctor had urged Captain Barclay to leave Fort Malden and attack the Americans. Proctor reasoned quite correctly that the more time Perry had to strengthen his fleet, the weaker the British position on the lake would become. On the sunny morning of September 10, Barclay, who had been delaying because of supply problems, reluctantly maneuvered his fleet toward the American squadron at Put-in-Bay. Excited at the prospect of battle, Perry decided that Elliott's *Niagara* would face the *Lady Charlotte,* while the *Lawrence* would do battle with the *Detroit.*

At first, the wind blew the British ships directly at Perry's fleet. But about 10:00 A.M., the breezes shifted, allowing Perry to get the weather gauge and bear down on Barclay's fleet. At 11:45 the British opened fire on the approaching *Lawrence,* initiating the battle. As the two flagships—*Detroit* and *Lawrence*—blasted away at each other, the American gunboats glided in and out of the fray, crossing in front of the bows of the British ships and raking them with cannon fire. Meanwhile, the Kentucky marksmen on the American vessels showered musket fire onto the decks of the enemy ships. As planned, Elliott tried to engage the *Lady Charlotte,* but the British vessel kept its distance.

At first, neither fleet gained a definite advantage. Then, shortly after 12:30 P.M., the *Lady Charlotte* broke away from the *Niagara* and joined the *Detroit* in a ferocious assault on Perry's *Lawrence.* Seeing their chance to destroy the Americans' lead ship, nearly all of the British vessels moved in, opened fire on the *Lawrence,* and in the following moments shot it nearly to pieces. "Judge the scene at 1:22 P.M.," Perry's sailing master, William Taylor, later wrote,

---

A Doctor Recalls the Lake Battle

This is a brief extract from the account of the Lake Erie Battle penned by U.S. surgeon Usher Parsons shortly afterward (quoted in volume 2 of Dudley's Naval War of 1812).

"About 12 o'clock on a clear pleasant day we met the enemy. The action soon became general and was severely felt, especially on board the *Lawrence,* the flag ship. . . . The vessels being shallow built, afforded no . . . place of shelter [so] the wounded were . . . received on the wardroom floor. . . . Our prospects . . . darkened; every new visitor from the deck bringing tidings still more dismal. . . . But this state of despair was short. The commodore [Oliver Perry] was still unhurt, had gone on board the *Niagara* and with the small vessels bearing down upon the enemy soon brought down the flags of [i.e., defeated] their two heaviest ships and thus changed the horrors of defeat into shouts of victory."

Oliver Perry's superior leadership abilities and his refusal to give up lent inspiration and determination to his men.

when 22 Men & officers lay dead on the decks & 66 wounded, every gun dismounted, carriages knocked to pieces—every strand of rigging cut off—masts & spars shot & tottering over head & in fact an unmanageable wreck. . . . Not another gun could be *worked* or *fired* or *manned*.[41]

At this point, it appeared to many on both sides that the Americans had lost the battle. But Perry, perhaps remembering Lawrence's dying words, refused to admit defeat. He grabbed the blue flag bearing Lawrence's last message, jumped into a cutter, and rowed feverishly for the *Niagara*, which fortunately was headed in his direction. All the while, British gunboats chased him, firing both cannon and muskets at his tiny craft. As the missiles whizzed and splashed around him, Perry caught sight of the American gunboats *Scorpion, Porcupine,* and *Tigress* speeding to his rescue; luckily for him, they chased off the British vessels, allowing him to climb aboard and take charge of the *Niagara*.

The British were sure that, once aboard the *Niagara*, Perry would turn tail and run, acknowledging defeat. This would have been a relief, for the British fleet was in poor shape, with two of its ships disabled and burning and several others damaged. Moreover, most of the British officers had died in the furious exchanges of cannon and musket fire, and Captain Barclay was badly wounded. The British were both surprised and disconcerted to see that Perry had not given up and that the *Niagara*, accompanied by the American gunboats, was bearing down on them at full speed. Desperately and often gallantly, the British sailors tried to maneuver their ships away, but it was no use. The *Niagara*, with Perry screaming orders from the foredeck, savagely raked the remaining British vessels.

The Americans in Control of the Lake

At 3:00 P.M., the British lowered their flags, admitting defeat. Perry ran his own flag back up the mast of the *Lawrence*, which brought a loud cheer from his exhausted men. Losses were heavy on both sides. Twenty-seven Americans were dead, twenty-two of whom were from the *Lawrence*, and ninety-six Americans were wounded; forty-one British were killed and ninety-four wounded. Most of the British ships, like the American *Lawrence*, were beyond repair.

Before Perry could take a well-deserved rest, he had one more important task to perform. General Harrison, with a force of several thousand men, was waiting for word of the outcome of the lake battle. Harrison realized that if the Americans won control of the lakes, the land advantage in the war would shift in his favor because Perry's ships could then ferry Harrison's troops to any point in southern Canada and also keep his army well supplied. Perry pulled an old envelope from his pocket and scratched out a note for Harrison. A day later, one of Perry's men rode into the American general's camp and handed him the message. Harrison smiled broadly when he read the following words:

> CAPTAIN OLIVER H. PERRY TO MAJOR GENERAL WILLIAM HENRY HARRISON, U.S.A. We have met the enemy and they are ours: Two ships, two brigs, one schooner, & one sloop. Yours with great respect and esteem, O. H. PERRY.[42]

After Perry's victory, British control of the entire Lake Erie region suddenly collapsed. Proctor's supplies had nearly run out and his troops, including the Indians and their families, were on the verge of starvation. Fort Malden was defenseless because Barclay had stripped it of its cannon for use on the *Detroit*. So there was nothing left to do but abandon the lake forts and retreat overland toward British strongholds far to the east. Proctor's evacuation was far too slow and disorganized, however. He did not realize that Harrison's forces were already moving on Fort Malden.

Proctor also failed to anticipate the mood of the approaching American soldiers. For the first time in the war, U.S. ground troops were passionately motivated and spurred on by a single goal. The massacre of their former comrades, Winchester and his men, at the Raisin River was still fresh in their memory. And they wanted revenge.

Chapter

5 Mortal Combat on the Frontier

The American victory on Lake Erie changed the balance of power in the northwest region of the United States. The British lost their hold over the area and could no longer effectively supply their Indian allies. But the danger to American settlers was far from over, for the hostile Indian tribes that had been incited and armed by the British still posed a threat to many sectors of the western and southern frontiers. And even as the British withdrew, some tribes continued to attack the white Americans. The British hoped that these uprisings would divert American resources and manpower away from the larger struggle with British troops. In fact, Britain badly needed this diversion because most of its soldiers and supplies had to be used in the war against France, and it could make only a limited commitment of men and arms to the North American conflict.

In fighting back against the British-inspired Indians, the Americans had two principal goals. The most obvious was to defeat the Indians as part of the overall war effort against Britain. The other goal had important consequences and benefits for the future of the United States, namely that conquering the native tribes along the frontier would ensure faster and easier expansion of white American settlement into the western territories. Of course, it was inevitable that this policy would worsen the already strained relations between the whites and most Indians. Therefore, the war with Britain not only intensified white–Indian tensions and hatreds, but also established a pattern in which the whites would continue to take Native American lands as the country expanded westward.

Still, not all of the Indians went to war with the white settlers. During the course of the conflict, some tribes, such as the Choctaw in Louisiana and Mississippi, actually helped the United States fight other tribes. And a few tribes, like the Wyandot in the Great Lakes region, started out fighting the white Americans, then switched sides and helped them. American troops referred to these as "friendly" Indians. The sad fact is that the friendly Indians sincerely believed that these Americans would later reward them by allowing them to keep their own ancestral hunting grounds. Eventually, however, even those Native Americans who

THE CUSTOM OF SCALPING

Scalping, the removal of part or all of the scalp, along with the hair, was practiced by numerous North American Indian tribes in frontier warfare; however, the custom was most common among the Indians in the eastern and southern United States. For example, the Creek and Choctaw Indians, who inhabited the region bordering the Gulf of Mexico, believed that a young man had to take a scalp to qualify as a full-fledged warrior. They also thought that their ancestors' spirits could not rest in peace unless enemy scalps adorned their lodges. By contrast, most midwestern Indians saw scalping as less important, viewing stealing an enemy's horse or touching his living body better tests for warriors because such acts took more courage.

The practice of scalping became more widespread among the Indians in the 1700s because of the influence of white European settlers, who introduced firearms, which caused more deaths and, therefore, more opportunities for scalping. The whites also introduced metal knives, which made the practice easier and more efficient. In addition, the French, Spanish, British, and Dutch all offered bounties of money and other valuables to Indians in exchange for scalps of both Indian and white enemies. It should be emphasized that Indians were not the only practitioners of scalping; many white trappers and frontiersmen also scalped their enemies.

In this illustration, two Indians prepare to scalp a white pioneer woman.

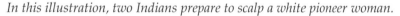

aided the United States against Britain would end up being pushed aside by white civilization's relentless westward march.

TECUMSEH CONFRONTS PROCTOR

In 1812, when the war with Britain began, there were few friendly Indians allied with the United States. Most of the tribes inhabiting the huge frontier stretching from Canada to the Gulf of Mexico opposed the Americans; and several of them looked for inspiration to Tecumseh, the great Shawnee chief who had devoted himself to stopping white westward expansion. It was only natural, therefore, that Tecumseh and the British, who also wanted to contain the Americans, became allies. In September 1813, writes noted English historian John Sugden, Tecumseh

> was about forty-five years of age and at the zenith of his power. . . . In the British alliance he saw his last opportunity to save the lands of his people. Encouraged by British promises of support for Indian claims, he had worked with energy and determination to convince the warriors that only with British assistance could they defeat the United States.[43]

While Oliver Perry and Robert Barclay did battle for mastery of Lake Erie, Tecumseh and his people were camped near Fort Malden. Although they were too far away from the fighting to see the ships, the Indians could hear the thunder of the cannon in the distance. Tecumseh was well aware that the British considered maintaining control of the lakes their top priority; but he was more interested in fighting the Americans on land, for in his view, it was land, specifically Indian land, that was most at stake. The British had promised him they would help fight for that land, so he was surprised when, following the lake battle, the British hastily began preparing to abandon Fort Malden.

As Colonel Proctor packed his personal belongings, Tecumseh confronted him. The chief demanded to know why the British were leaving. Surely, he said, they would not abandon the area and their Indian allies after losing merely one battle. "You told us," he reminded Proctor,

> to bring forward our families to this place and we did so. And you promised to take care of them and they should want for nothing while the men would go and fight the enemy—that we were not to trouble ourselves with the enemy's garrisons [forts] . . . and that our Father [i.e., the British commander] would attend to that part of the business. You also told your red children that you would take care of your garrison here, which made our hearts glad. . . . Our fleet has gone out. . . . We have heard the great guns . . . and we are much astonished to see our Father tying up everything and preparing to run [away].[44]

The chief was clearly upset. This worried Proctor because he desperately needed Tecumseh and his warriors to help protect the British retreat, and if the

Tecumseh confronts his ally, General Proctor, during their retreat, demanding that the British leader stand and fight the Americans.

chief thought the British were cowards, he might turn his back on his white allies. Sure enough, the charge of cowardice came next from Tecumseh's lips:

> You always told us to remain here and take care of our lands; it made our hearts glad to hear that was your wish. Our Great Father, the King, is the head and you represent him. You always told us that you would never draw your foot off British ground; but now, Father, we see you are drawing back, and we are sorry to see our Fa-

ther doing so, without seeing the enemy. We must compare our Father's conduct to a fat animal that carries its tail upon its back; but when affrighted, it drops it between its legs and runs off.[45]

"WE SHALL NEVER RETURN"

Luckily for Proctor, several of Tecumseh's fellow chiefs convinced him not to abandon the British. The Indians had given the British their word, they said, and it would be wrong to break a promise. Taking advantage of this opening, Proctor assured Tecumseh that his warriors would be able to fight the Americans later at a better time and place. The chief decided to give his white ally the benefit of the doubt and, with much reluctance, ordered his people to dismantle their lodges and prepare to depart. On September 23, 1813, the Indians watched with great sadness as Proctor's men set fire to the fort (to deprive the Americans of its use). "We are now going to follow the British," Tecumseh was heard to say quietly, "and I feel certain that we shall never return."[46] Great plumes of black smoke curled into the sky as some eight hundred British and twelve hundred Indians began their solemn retreat northeastward toward the Thames River.

Meanwhile, unaware that the British were withdrawing, William Henry Harrison organized his men for an assault on Fort Malden. Harrison's army of five thousand had joined forces with thirty-five hundred Kentucky riflemen under General Isaac Shelby and one thousand

Tecumseh: An "Uncommon Genius"

Tecumseh's greatness as a leader is still not fully appreciated by non-Indians, perhaps because he and other Native Americans ultimately ended up on the losing side. No one knew his qualities better than his archenemy, future president William Henry Harrison, who paid the chief this tribute after the two met twice at Vincennes, capital of the Indiana Territory. This excerpt is from Colbert's Eyewitness to America.

"The implicit obedience and respect which the followers of Tecumseh pay to him is really astonishing, and more than any other circumstance bespeaks him [shows him to be] one of those uncommon geniuses which spring up occasionally to produce revolutions, and overturn the established order of things. If it were not for the vicinity [closeness] of the United States [to his and other Indian lands], he would, perhaps, be the founder of an empire that would rival in glory Mexico [i.e., the Maya and Aztecs] or Peru [i.e., the Incas]. No difficulties deter him. For four years he has been in constant motion. You see him today on the Wabash [River], and in a short time hear of him on the shores of Lake Erie or Michigan, or on the banks of the Mississippi; and wherever he goes he makes an impression favorable to his circumstances."

This imposing statue of the great Indian leader Tecumseh stands on the grounds of the U.S. Naval Academy at Annapolis.

During the War of 1812, William Henry Harrison commanded the U.S. ground troops in the northwestern frontier. He later became the ninth president of the United States.

cavalry commanded by Colonel Richard Johnson. Harrison ordered Johnson to ride his men around the lakeshore and move on the rear of the fort, while the rest of the army took full advantage of its new mastery of the lake. Harrison had Perry move the American troops by ship to a point just south of the fort, completing in a few days an operation that normally would have involved an overland trek of at least two weeks.

When the American forces converged on Fort Malden on September 26, they found a charred pile of rubble, parts of which were still smoldering. But Harrison was encouraged rather than disappointed by the spectacle, for in his view Proctor's hasty retreat indicated that the British

were in a weakened state and afraid of combat. Accordingly, the American commander rallied his forces to chase the British. Johnson's cavalry crossed the Detroit River and galloped overland, while Perry's ships carried Harrison and a large contingent of his army along the lake toward the Thames.

TECUMSEH'S GIFT

As the Americans mobilized, the British continued their slow and poorly organized retreat miles to the east. Morale was low, partly because Proctor seemed more interested in his own needs and comfort than in the condition of his troops. The Indians were dejected too. Tecumseh's people repeatedly told him that there was no honor in this retreat and that they would rather turn and face the Americans, no matter what the outcome. On October 4, Tecumseh once again accused Proctor of cowardice, reminding him that the British had broken their promises to the Indians. The chief informed the British leader that they must now turn and make a stand against the Americans; otherwise, the Indians would follow the British no farther.

At the same moment that Proctor received this ultimatum, he was informed that the Americans had captured his supply boats only a few miles to his rear and were approaching fast. Grimly, Proctor realized that he no longer had any choice: He would have to fight. With darkness setting in, he camped his forces beside the Thames, at a spot near the future site of Thamesville.

That night, Tecumseh sat silently beside his fire. A young warrior, who went by the name of Billy Caldwell, approached him and asked, "Father, what are we to do? Shall we fight the Americans?" Tecumseh nodded, saying, "Yes, my son, on the morrow, we will be in their smoke [given off by their muskets]." The chief then gathered his people around him and announced, "My children, hear me well. Tomorrow we go to our final battle with the Americans. In this battle I will be killed."[47] There was a gasp from the listeners. No one knew how the great chief was able to predict his own death, but none doubted the prophecy, for over the years he had correctly foreseen many victories and other happenings, and they accepted that he had a gift for seeing into the future.

"You are my friends, my people," Tecumseh continued. "I love you too well to see you sacrificed in an unequal contest from which no good can result." There was an added touch of sadness in his voice when he said,

> I would dissuade you from fighting this fight, encourage you to leave now, this night, for there is no victory ahead, only sorrow. Yet . . . you have made known to me that it is your desire to fight the Americans here and I am willing to go with my people and be guided by their wishes.[48]

Tecumseh then gave away all of his possessions to his family and friends, as was the custom of many Indians who suspected they were dying. Afterward, he once more sat silently before his fire; and out of respect, no one disturbed him.

SLAUGHTER ON THE THAMES

In the afternoon of October 5, 1813, in preparation for battle, Henry Proctor formed a defensive line near the river. On the left side of the line he placed his British regulars and on the right side Tecumseh's Native American forces. At a little past three o'clock, all watched in grave silence as the much larger U.S. Army approached to within several hundred yards.

Then the American bugles signaling the charge pierced the air, breaking the silence, and, following Harrison's preset plan, Richard Johnson led his horsemen directly at the British regulars. At the head of one of his detachments rode Oliver Perry, seemingly as much at home on a horse as on a ship's foredeck. Shouts of "Remember the River Raisin" could be heard over the din of musket fire and pounding horses' hooves. Seconds later, the wave of men and animals smashed with devastating force into and through the British lines. The British soldiers were able to get off only a single round of musket fire, for as they rushed to reload, hundreds of Americans wielding pistols and tomahawks pounced on and overwhelmed them, forcing them to retreat in confusion. Proctor rode back and forth attempting to rally his frightened troops. "For shame men!" he shouted. "What are you running away for?"[49] But his words were largely drowned out by the noise of battle, and a few seconds later he joined in the stampede of fleeing men.[50]

At that same moment, Harrison led his foot soldiers in a frontal assault on the Indian lines. As a consequence of the rapid British retreat, Johnson was able to regroup his horsemen and attack the Indians from the rear. Tecumseh's warriors fought bravely, but they were surrounded and hopelessly outnumbered; and as a group of American marksmen emptied their muskets into the Indian ranks, the great chief fell dead. Seeing his demise, his remaining warriors lost heart and abruptly fell back and disappeared into the deep woods.

The battle that Harrison and his men had been itching to fight for so long had lasted less than five minutes. Seven Americans had been killed and twenty-two wounded, while the British counted eighteen dead, twenty-five wounded, and more than six hundred captured. Only thirty-three Indian bodies were found, but Harrison was sure that the retreating warriors had carried away several of their dead. Hoping to identify Tecumseh's remains, the Americans called on Simon Kenton, an old frontier scout who had known the Shawnee chief. But Kenton, who admired and respected Tecumseh, purposely pointed out the wrong body.

Richard Johnson (in foreground, mounted) charges his cavalry toward the Indian allies of the British. Vastly outnumbered, the Indian opposition quickly collapsed.

An American Meets His End

John Richardson, a volunteer in Harrison's army, later penned this graphic account of one of the many horrific moments in the battle beside the Thames. (excerpted from Tecumseh's Last Stand *by John Sugden).*

"An American rifleman who had been dismounted within a few paces of the spot where I stood was fired at by three warriors. . . . The unfortunate man received the several [musket] balls in his body, yet, though faint and tottering . . . made every exertion to save himself. The foremost of his pursuers . . . threw his tomahawk . . . with such force and precision that it . . . opened the skull. . . . Laying down his rifle, he [the Indian] drew . . . his knife, and . . . proceeded to make a circular incision throughout the scalp. This done, he grasped the bloody instrument between his teeth, and placing his knees on the back of his victim, while. . . [grasping] the hair, the scalp was torn off without much apparent difficulty. . . . All this was the work of a minute."

Soldiers then stripped the corpse, scalped it, and cut strips of skin from the arms, legs, cheeks, and other fleshy areas to make souvenir pouches and belts.

Andrew Jackson and the Creek War

Tecumseh's dreams of a federation of all the frontier tribes died with him. But even in death he remained an inspiration to many Indians who hated and distrusted the white Americans, and in the months following the Thames battle a number of tribes launched offensives. The largest and most famous of these uprisings was that of the Creeks, who inhabited sections of Georgia, Alabama, and Florida. The American government reacted quickly to the Creek threat, partly because it wanted to protect the thousands of white settlers who lived in the southern states and territories. There was also the fear that the Creeks might join forces with other tribes along the coast of the Gulf of Mexico. The British would surely take advantage of this situation and ally themselves with the tribes; and with thousands of Indians to support them, they could more easily attack New Orleans and other towns on the gulf.

The American offensive against the Creeks was led by Major General Andrew Jackson, of the Tennessee militia. A tall, imposing, and dynamic individual, Jackson had already gained fame as a local politician and Indian fighter. One of his hallmarks, now and in later years, was that his men were usually more afraid of him than they were of the enemy. Illustrative of his disciplinarian, no-nonsense attitude was an incident during the Creek War in which one of his young militiamen refused to obey an order; Jackson had him court-martialed and shot, the first such execution since the Revolution. "An army cannot exist where order and subordination are wholly disregarded,"[51]

A provocative woodcut on an American wartime circular stirs up fear and hatred of the frontier Indian "menace."

the general (who later became known as "Old Hickory") declared afterward.

The Creeks also felt Jackson's wrath. Between November 1813 and March 1814 his forces repeatedly attacked and defeated them. The Indians offered tough, courageous resistance but were ultimately overcome by the whites' superior numbers and weapons. In late March 1814, some twelve hundred Creeks made a desperate last stand at Horseshoe Bend, on the Tallapoosa River in Alabama. After several hours of bloody hand-to-hand combat, almost all of the Creek men were killed, and Jackson took about three hundred Indian women and children prisoner. The victory was so decisive that a few months later the Creeks acknowledged total defeat and had to give half of their lands, about 23 million acres, to the United States.

The Creeks' tragedy turned out to be a stroke of good fortune for the American war effort. As U.S. leaders had feared, the British tried to incite and arm the Creeks as part of a campaign against the country's southern flank. Unfortunately for the British, though, they waited too long to forge an alliance with the Creeks; Jackson's win at Horseshoe Bend deprived Britain of a potentially powerful and strategically valuable ally in the war's southern theater.

YOUNGER, MORE VIGOROUS MEN

By the spring of 1814, many Americans felt confident that they would triumph over the British. True, the U.S. economy was in poor shape, and some parts of the country, notably New England, continued to oppose and contribute little to the war effort, increasing the financial strain. Yet American forces had engaged the British and Indians in mortal combat in various parts of the northwestern and southern frontiers and managed to emerge victorious, bringing these areas largely under American control. Many of the settlers who had earlier fled returned to their homes, and thousands more headed west to occupy the lands recently won from the Indians.

Most of the credit for the recent American successes belonged to young, energetic, and talented field commanders like Perry, Harrison, and Jackson. President Madison continued to replace the older generals, whom one historian calls "the worst military leaders of any war in which the United States has ever been engaged,"[52] with younger, more vigorous men. And as he did so, troop morale improved and enlistments rose. By May 1814 there were about forty thousand men in uniform, a full third more than a year before.

Hopes of a speedy victory over the enemy soon began to fade, however. Early in 1814, the British and their European allies decisively defeated Napoleon, finally bringing the long war with France to a close. The British could now devote many

During the War of 1812, Indians, most of whom were allied to the British, staged repeated attacks on white settlements.

Both as a general and later as president, Andrew Jackson was a well-known figure during the early years of the United States and as the country expanded westward.

more troops, ships, and supplies to the American conflict. Before, the British had viewed the North American war as little more than a minor diversion; now, the strongest nation on earth was ready to direct its full resources to punishing the insolent Americans. Hereafter, U.S. naval officer Joseph Nicholson correctly surmised, the Americans would be fighting "not for free trade and sailors' rights, not for the conquest of Canada, but for our national existence."[53]

Chapter

6 Washington in Flames

France's defeat drastically changed the nature of the war between the United States and Great Britain. Although the Americans had suffered numerous setbacks in the war's early months, U.S. prospects had later improved markedly, thanks largely to Perry's, Harrison's, and Jackson's victories on the frontiers. With the war in Europe now over, however, the British began to concentrate all their energies and resources against the United States, threatening in effect to nullify recent American successes.

President Madison and other American leaders worried about this new turn of events, and rightly so. Most of them now realized that it had perhaps been foolish to pass up earlier opportunities to make peace with Britain. In the summer of 1812, for instance, when the news of the suspension of the Orders in Council arrived, the U.S. government could have canceled its war declaration and pursued diplomacy. But the war hawks had insisted on fighting, mainly in hopes of getting their hands on Canada.

The second lost chance for peace had come early in 1813, when the United States seemed to be winning the war. The British, still occupied with the French, had seemed willing to negotiate, but the Americans had stubbornly insisted that there could be no peace until Britain stopped impressing U.S. sailors. The British had countered that if the United States would stop fighting, they would

This poem was written to commemorate the death of Robert Howel, an American sailor impressed by the British and forced to fight against his countrymen.

consider ending impressment. But American leaders had refused to compromise on the matter.

Now, in 1814, with the United States facing Britain's full military might, Madison was ready to do more than compromise. He sent negotiators to tell British leaders that he had dropped the impressment issue as a condition of peace. But it was too late. The victory over Napoleon had given the British people new confidence and made them rethink their approach to the American conflict. One of Madison's diplomats, Albert Gallatin, wrote home from Britain, "The whole nation is delirious with joy. . . . They thirst for great revenge and will not be satisfied without it."[54] There was certainly no mystery about where this desire for retribution would now be directed. "Now that the tyrant [Napoleon] Bonaparte has been consigned to infamy," the London *Times* stated in April 1814,

> there is no public feeling in this country stronger than that of indignation against the Americans. . . . That it [the U.S.] should have attempted to plunge the parricidal [father-killing] weapon into the heart of that country from whence its own origin was derived . . . [is] so loathsome, so hateful, that it naturally stirs up the indignation that we have described.[55]

In this hostile atmosphere, the British refused even to talk about bargaining. Realizing that they now enjoyed a huge military advantage, they prepared to cross the Atlantic and bring their former subjects back into their global dominion.

BRITAIN'S INVASION PLAN

The new British strategy consisted of a three-pronged assault on the United States. One part of the assault was to be an attack on the largest U.S. coastal cities, beginning with the national capital, Washington, D.C., and including Baltimore, Maryland; Charleston, South Carolina; and Savannah, Georgia. This operation was intended to achieve two goals. First, it would divert U.S. troops and supplies away from the New York assault, and second, it would, the British hoped, frighten, embarrass, and break the spirit of the American people.

Another invasion force would move down Lake Champlain and attack New York State from the north, the object being to split the nation in half, separating New England from the rest of the country.[56] The British knew that there was still a great deal of opposition to the war in the New England states, where many people viewed the conflict as unwinnable and a useless drain on American money and resources. Once New York fell, British leaders reasoned, New England could be convinced to rejoin the former mother country. The other U.S. states would then easily go down to defeat.

The third thrust of the British assault was aimed at the gulf coast, beginning with the largest and most important southern city—New Orleans. Located at the mouth of the mighty Mississippi River, New Orleans was the key to control of river shipping, and the British correctly concluded that capturing the city would cut off all commerce moving north into the western frontier. Yet there was an even more important

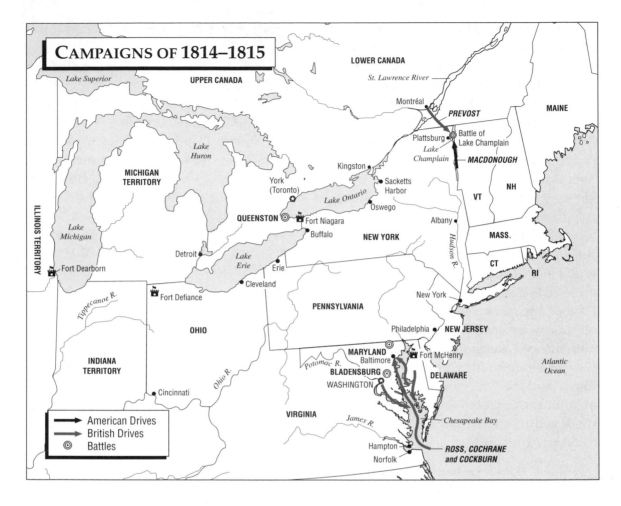

strategic reason for taking New Orleans. Commanding the Mississippi would eventually ensure Britain's mastery of the vast territories of the Louisiana Purchase, through which the river flowed. The British would then have a firm foothold in North America, one rich in farmland, timber, furs, and other resources.

OUT FOR REVENGE

By July 1814, the British were nearly ready to put their grand invasion plan into effect. The army-navy assault on the coastal cities would strike first, under the direction of Admiral Alexander Cochrane. At the outset, Cochrane planned only to capture the cities, not destroy them; however, he changed his mind in mid-July after receiving a letter from General George Prevost, who was still in command of the British forces in Canada. Prevost described how American troops had unnecessarily looted and burned some Canadian towns near Lake Erie. These actions had not been authorized by American commanders, who sent Prevost an apology; but because it took so long for the messenger to travel across the frontier, the apology arrived after Prevost had already written to Cochrane. Prevost asked his colleague to "assist in inflicting the measure of retaliation which shall deter the enemy from a repetition of similar outrages." Cochrane agreed to make his own operation, at least in part, a revenge raid. He informed his troops, "You are hereby required and directed to destroy and lay waste [to] such towns and districts upon the coasts as you may find assailable [easy targets]."[57]

In early August 1814, Cochrane's fleet arrived at Chesapeake Bay, the large waterway separating the coastal sections of Virginia and Maryland. Baltimore, one of the prime British targets, lay near the bay's northern shore, and Washington, another important objective, lay between the Potomac and Patuxent Rivers, both of which flow into the bay. Cochrane's forces were formidable, consisting of four huge ships of the line and twenty frigates and sloops. He also had twenty troop transport ships, carrying more than four thousand battle-hardened troops.

The only American ships defending Chesapeake Bay at that time were fifteen small gunboats commanded by Commodore Joshua Barney. Realizing that his tiny craft had no chance against the British fleet, Barney retreated up the Patuxent. After conferring with his chief officers, General Robert Ross and Admiral George Cockburn, Cochrane decided to chase and attempt to capture Barney's boats before moving on the cities. To this end, Ross landed troops on the shore of the Patuxent. While Cochrane's ships pursued Barney along the river, Ross and his men marched ahead and took a position behind the American boats; and by

A WARNING THAT MIGHT HAVE SAVED THE CAPITAL

Well after the British attack on Washington, D.C., in late August 1814, U.S. officials discovered a letter (excerpted here from Lord's The Dawn's Early Light*), dated July 27 and addressed to President Madison. Apparently written by an impressed American seaman on a British ship and smuggled ashore, it had reached the White House by August 4, but the overworked president had never gotten around to reading it.*

"Your enemy have in agitation an attack on the capital of the United States. The manner in which they intend doing it is to take the advantage of a fair wind in ascending the Patuxent [River]; and after having ascended it a certain distance, to land their men at once, and to make all possible dispatch to the capital; batter it down, and then return to their vessels immediately. In doing this there is calculated to be employed upwards of seven thousand men. The time of this designed attack I do not know."

August 22 Barney was trapped. Rather than allow his boats to fall into the enemy's hands, he blew them up. The way was now clear for the British to attack either Washington or Baltimore; and they chose Washington.

PANIC IN THE CAPITAL

At this fateful juncture, the capital of the United States was nearly defenseless. The Americans had expected the British to strike at Baltimore first, so U.S. commanders had failed to prepare adequate barricades and other defenses around the capital. Fewer than two thousand soldiers were available to defend Washington and its surrounding settlements. Making matters worse, nearby states refused to send their militias to aid the city; when General William Winder, the officer in charge of the city's defenses, asked for three thousand troops from these states, he got only about three hundred. This brought an angry reaction from Madison, who issued an emergency order, forcing Maryland's governor to dispatch two thousand soldiers to the capital.

On August 23, General Ross's forces marched westward from the Patuxent toward Washington, about fifteen miles away. Hearing that the British were approaching, most of the citizens of the capital panicked, and people fought over horses, wagons, and carts to carry them and their possessions out of the city. Many families boarded up their houses and buried their valuables before fleeing.

While the president helped organize defenses, back at the White House the nation's personable, witty, and resourceful first lady, Dolley Madison, tried to save some of the mansion's priceless artifacts. Among other objects hastily packed was the now famous portrait of George Washington painted by Gilbert Stuart. On August 23, she wrote to her sister, "I am still here within sound of the cannon! Mr. Madison comes not; may God protect him. Two messengers covered with dust come to bid me fly."[58] (After escaping, Mrs. Madison stopped at a farmhouse to rest and was there accosted by the lady of the house, who screamed, "Your husband has got mine out fighting, and

First Lady Dolley Madison was known for her wit and charm. Madison was responsible for saving valuable articles from the White House before it was burned to the ground.

damn you, you shan't stay in my house! So get out!"[59] The woman many considered the perfect hostess had been driven from two homes in one day.)

THE BLADENSBURG RACES

Meanwhile, General Winder rushed all available soldiers to the nearby town of Bladensburg, through which the British would have to pass to enter Washington. Madison and his cabinet members, including Secretary of State (and future president) James Monroe, galloped into Bladensburg on the morning of August 24, ready to take the field and fight if needed. A few minutes later, the troops from Maryland arrived, bringing the total of the U.S. forces to just over five thousand. Even though their numbers were now greater than the enemy's, the Americans, having rushed to the scene from every direction, were confused, disorganized, and exhausted.

At about 1:00 P.M., the British appeared on the other side of the river and surveyed the scene. In their eyes, the Americans seemed not only unprepared for battle but also unworthy opponents. Most of the American troops, a British officer observed, "seemed [like] country people, who would have been much more appropriately employed in attending to their agricultural occupations, than in standing with their muskets in their hands."[60]

Wasting no time, the British attacked what they viewed as a contemptible collection of rabble. At first, the American lines held firm. But when the British be-

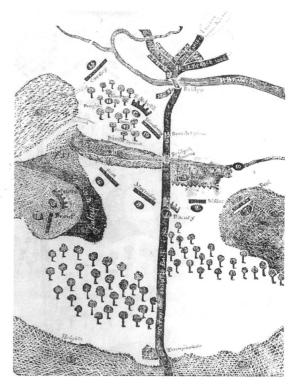

A contemporary map of the Battle of Bladensburg. The British had to pass through Bladensburg in order to attack the capital.

gan firing Congreve rockets (small projectiles not much larger or more harmful than ordinary fireworks), the American horses and pack mules took flight, and so did most of the American troops, who, never before having encountered rockets, feared they might be lethal. As the bulk of the army fled, one low-ranking officer ran so fast that he fell down dead from exhaustion. Madison, Monroe, Winder, and the other American top brass knew that the rockets were harmless, but it was too late. The president and his cabinet had no choice but to join the mad flight, which later earned the contemptuous name the "Bladensburg Races."

THE CONGREVE ROCKET

By the 1600s, Europeans, including the French, Germans, and Poles, had begun using rockets in battle. Most of these devices were small and posed no threat to soldiers except in the case of a direct hit; and since they were wildly inaccurate, there were few direct hits. So they were mainly used to set fire to buildings or ships' sails or to scare away enemy horses and pack animals.

In the early 1790s, Haidar Ali, an Indian prince, invented a twelve-pound rocket with a range of one and a half miles. He fired thousands of these weapons at the British in India, inflicting much fire damage and several casualties. Surprised and impressed, a British army officer, William Congreve, developed similar rockets that afterward bore his name.

In a mass rocket attack in 1807, the British fired twenty-five thousand of the devices at Copenhagen, Denmark, burning the city to the ground. And on August 24, 1814, hoping to frighten U.S. pack mules, the British fired a few Congreve rockets at the Americans at Bladensburg. The terrified American soldiers fled, leaving Washington, D.C., open to capture.

THE CITY RANSACKED

That evening, General Ross and Admiral Cockburn led their troops into Washington, which by now was largely deserted. They immediately set fire to the U.S. Capitol building, then made their way through the silent streets to the White House. Dolley Madison and her servants were nowhere to be found, but it was obvious that they had fled only a short time before, since the dining room table was set, and lamb, chicken, and vegetables were cooking in the kitchen. Pleasantly surprised by the scene, the British officers sat down and ate supper. Then they burned the White House and moved on.

In the next few hours, the British continued to burn and ransack the city. They torched the navy yard, the War and Treasury buildings, the Library of Congress, and the office of the city's largest newspaper, the *National Intelligencer*.[61] From their position in the surrounding hills, American leaders, troops, and civilians watched the fire's flickering red glow dance against the clouds. Attorney General Richard Rush later recalled, "If at intervals the dismal sight was lost to our view, we got it again from some hilltop . . . where we paused to look at it."[62] Some of the watchers swore angrily. Others wept. And all felt helpless. That night a violent thunderstorm put out the flames, but the damage had been done, for the national capital had already been reduced to a charred pile of ruins.

THE DAWN'S EARLY LIGHT

After capturing and burning Washington so easily, the British were confident that they would have little trouble taking the next city—Baltimore. They expected to sail their warships into the harbor, which was protected by Fort McHenry, destroy the fort with cannon fire, then land troops for a frontal assault on the city. But this time their plan did not go so smoothly. The British attack on the capital had given the Americans time to fortify Baltimore, where more than sixteen thousand U.S. troops were now concentrated. Aided by thousands of civilians, they built barricades and sank dozens of boats to block the harbor.

The British moved on Baltimore on September 12 and immediately encountered difficulties. When General Ross tried to attack by land, he was killed and his troops were driven back by the defenders; at the

British soldiers march through the streets of the American capital, burning many of the major buildings, including the White House.

same time, the British vessels entering the harbor could not get past the barrier of sunken boats. They did bombard Fort McHenry from a distance during the night of September 13, managing to lob more than eighteen hundred cannonballs into it. A Washington lawyer named Francis Scott Key witnessed the bombardment from a boat about eight miles away, occasionally catching glimpses of the "bright stripes and bright stars" of the fort's flag lit up by the "rockets' red glare." Moved by the scene, he jotted down his impressions on the back of a letter, creating what would later become the national anthem.[63]

In the morning, "by the dawn's early light," both Key and the British observed that Fort McHenry, its flag still waving proudly from its ramparts, had somehow endured the unmerciful pounding. Cochrane now concluded that any further attempts to capture Baltimore would be

THE BRITISH DINE AT THE WHITE HOUSE

On August 24, 1814, during the sacking of Washington, British officers entered the White House. George R. Gleig, a British officer, later described the scene (quoted here from Colbert's Eyewitness to America*).*

"When the detachment sent out to destroy Mr. Madison's house entered his dining parlor, they found a dinner table spread and covers laid for forty guests. Several kinds of wine, in handsome, cut-glass decanters, were cooling on the sideboard; plate holders stood by the fireplace, filled with dishes and plates; knives, forks, and spoons were arranged for immediate use; in short, everything was ready for the entertainment of a ceremonious party . . . whilst in the kitchen . . . spits, loaded with joints [animal limbs] of various sorts, turned before the fire; pots, saucepans, and other culinary utensils stood upon the grate; and all the other requisites [requirements] for an elegant and substantial repast [feast] were exactly in a state which indicated that they had been lately . . . abandoned. You will readily imagine that these preparations were beheld by a party of hungry soldiers with no indifferent eye. An elegant dinner, even though considerably overdressed, was a luxury to which few of them, at least for some time back, had been accustomed, and . . . appeared peculiarly inviting. They sat down to it, therefore . . . and, having satisfied their appetites . . . they finished by setting fire to the house which so liberally had entertained them."

The British hurl cannonballs at Fort McHenry. The bombardment, which lasted through the night of September 13, 1814, inspired Francis Scott Key to write "The Star-Spangled Banner."

futile and withdrew his forces. The British sailed out of Chesapeake Bay, leaving the Americans the unenviable task of rebuilding the smoldering U.S. capital.

IN DIRE STRAITS

The first phase of the British three-pronged invasion had been only partly successful, and the second turned out to be even less so. On August 31, 1814, General Prevost led a large force of British troops down the length of Lake Champlain with the intention of capturing New York. But an American fleet commanded by Lieutenant Thomas Macdonough defeated the British, forcing them to retreat back into Canada.

In the meantime, the third phase of the British plan—the capture of New Orleans and the southern United States—was

Lieutenant Thomas Macdonough congratulates his men after their resounding defeat of British general Prevost's fleet on Lake Champlain.

about to begin. The British had assembled a large force of ships and troops for the operation and were confident of victory, partly because they knew that the Americans were in dire straits. Thanks to the accumulated effects of the prewar embargo and the great cost of running the war, the U.S. Treasury was almost out of money and the government on the verge of collapse. To fight the British on so many fronts, the country needed more troops, but enlistments were down again. Madison thought about imposing a draft, but the New England states threatened to secede if he did so. Just when it most needed strength and unity to beat back the foreign invader, the United States seemed to be crumbling from within.

Chapter

7 Triumph in New Orleans

Many Americans viewed it a painful certainty that New Orleans would fall to the British. There were, after all, only a few thousand U.S. troops, under Andrew Jackson's command, to defend the entire southern frontier, including the cities of Mobile and New Orleans. By December 1814, Admiral Cochrane, who had led the expedition against Washington, was ready to launch a large-scale attack on the American gulf coast. There seemed little hope that Jackson could repel the much larger British forces. Most American lawmakers worried that a defeat in the South would spell disaster for the country. And some of them stated openly that if the South came under Britain's control, Madison's already unpopular administration would surely topple.

THE COUNTRY IN A LOSE-LOSE SITUATION

Indeed, Madison was already in serious political trouble. Many blamed him for the poor planning that had led to the shameful sacking of Washington. And with practically no money in the Treasury,

he was unable to forge an army large enough to meet the new crisis. He had earlier called for creating a standing army of over sixty thousand men, but in the fall of 1814 only about half that number were

By the end of 1814, President Madison, pictured here, was in serious political trouble because of the worsening war situation.

serving in the military. Moreover, many of the troops were poorly equipped and supplied and had not been paid in months.

Madison also faced formidable and increasing opposition from the New England states, which had been against the war from the start. After the burning of the capital and with seemingly certain defeat in the South looming, their opposition became more vocal than ever. New England congressmen repeatedly called on the president to end the war by accepting whatever terms the British demanded; one Massachusetts legislator wanted his state to tell Madison "that he must either resign his office as President" or fire those of his advisers "who have . . . ruined the nation."[64]

THE HARTFORD CONVENTION

Tensions between New Englanders and the federal government further increased in November and December 1814, when the British seized about a hundred miles of Maine coastline, then part of Massachusetts. With a British attack on Boston apparently imminent, Massachusetts governor Caleb Strong agreed to call out the militia. However, he insisted that state officials, rather than federal army officers, lead the troops and also arrogantly demanded that Madison's government pay for his local militia. Madison staunchly refused to agree to either of these conditions.

Fuming, Governor Strong called a meeting of leaders from the New England states, which became known as the Hart-

ford Convention because it met in Hartford, Connecticut, in mid-December 1814. The delegates discussed the possibility of seceding from the Union and making their separate peace with Britain. Without their support, the rest of the country would not be strong enough to defend itself, and the British would surely be victorious. This was Madison's lowest ebb, in terms of both his public popularity and his personal emotional state. "I called on the President," wrote cabinet member William Wirt. "He looks miserably shattered and woe-begone. In short, he looked heartbroken. His mind is full of the New England sedition [rebellion]."[65]

Luckily for the country, the Hartford Convention's more moderate members gained control of the meeting. They put aside the idea of secession for the moment and proposed instead to do away with the national army. Under their plan, the states would defend themselves with their own troops, using money raised within their own borders. The federal government had always objected to this idea because of the danger of some states refusing to help a neighbor who was under attack; also, with many small separate armies and no federal control, it would be difficult, if not impossible, to coordinate an overall national defense. Ignoring these dangers, the delegates decided that if Congress did not go along with their demands, they would then meet again to consider seceding. In effect, their plan put Madison and the country in a lose-lose situation. If he agreed to eliminate the federal army, the national government could no longer defend the nation, and if he rejected the convention's demands, New England would secede, ensuring a British victory.

THE BRITISH CONFIDENT OF SUCCESS

As three messengers rode southward from Hartford in early January 1815 to present the convention's demands to the president, messengers of a very different sort sped northward from New Orleans. The momentous news they carried would ultimately overshadow the convention and forever silence New England's opposition to the war. New Orleans lies a thousand miles from Washington, D.C., and more than thirteen hundred miles from New England. In the early 1800s, messengers riding overland took as long as ten days to cover these distances, so the convention's delegates had no idea what had happened in the South during the Christmas and New Year's holidays.

In fact, the last news anyone had heard from New Orleans was that Admiral Cochrane's forces were assaulting the city. According to reliable reports, the British had fifty large warships, more than ten thousand men, and at least a thousand movable cannon, together composing the

The British forces that approached New Orleans had many movable cannon similar to those pictured here, which rest at the Jean Laffite National Historical Park and Preserve, in Chalmette, Louisiana.

biggest foreign force ever to move against a U.S. city. Not surprisingly, the British were quite confident of victory, prompting a contemporary American official to later write:

> Never did a fleet and army proceed towards their destination with higher hopes and in better spirits than the British expedition to New Orleans. So confident were they of success that a full set of civil officers to conduct the government of the territory accompanied the army. There was also a government editor and printing press to expound the policy and publish the orders and proceedings of the new government. There were many merchant ships in the squadron, which had been charted expressly to bear away the rich spoil that was expected to reward their capture and occupation of the city. . . . Hence the festivity and high-hearted jollity which enlivened the crowded decks of the British war vessels.[66]

JACKSON'S RAGTAG ARMY

Thus, like most other Americans, the New Englanders assumed that any further news from New Orleans would be bad. However, they had not reckoned on the ability of General Jackson to perform a veritable military miracle and turn certain defeat into triumph. Old Hickory had arrived on December 1, 1814, to begin fortifying the city, and he immediately set about strengthening the local forts, building barricades, and stationing soldiers at strategic sites. Of course, these measures were, by themselves, not nearly enough to stop the British, so he also began organizing the Louisiana militia and other local defenders.

The fighting force Jackson managed to piece together in less than three weeks was colorful to say the least, for it reflected the broad mix of cultures and nationalities that made up Louisiana's population at the time. A majority were descended from the French and Spanish who originally settled the area, but there were also fur trappers and frontiersmen, Choctaw and other local Indians, freed black slaves, and Creoles (people of mixed American and Spanish or French descent).

The ragtag army even included a group of pirates from the southern gulf coast, led by the personable, swashbuckling Jean Laffite. A few months before, the British had tried to get Laffite to join them against the Americans, promising that, in return, "you shall have the rank of Captain, lands will be given to you all in proportion to your respective ranks" and "your property shall be guaranteed to you, [and] your persons protected."[67] But Laffite and his men, who preyed mainly on Spanish ships, claimed to be loyal Americans and offered their services to Jackson. The American general was at first reluctant to deal with outlaws but soon decided that they "could not fail of being very useful"[68] to the cause. That cause received a further boost on December 23, when about twenty-five hundred volunteers from Tennessee arrived.

The Pirate Jean Laffite

Jean Laffite (ca. 1780–ca. 1825) was a colorful combination of pirate, smuggler, and patriot who aided the Americans in their defense of New Orleans against the British. Nothing is known about his early life. What is certain is that by 1810 he and his brother, Pierre, were in command of a band of smugglers based on the shore of Barataria Bay, south of New Orleans. The Laffites raided Spanish ships and sold the stolen goods on the thriving black market in New Orleans. Because they never attacked American ships and they contributed substantially to the local economy, U.S. authorities, despite branding them outlaws, usually left them alone.

In 1814, the British realized that Laffite and his pirates could be a valuable military asset in their conquest of the U.S. gulf coast. So British agents offered Jean Laffite $30,000 and a commission in the British navy if he helped them defeat the Americans. But the pirate, who had always claimed to be a loyal American patriot, refused the offer. He immediately sent the documents outlining the British proposal to the American authorities, along with a letter that read in part, "Though proscribed [outlawed] by my adopted country [the United States], I will never let slip any occasion of serving her or of proving that she has never ceased to be dear to me." (Quoted in Carter, *Blaze of Glory*, p. 46)

Soon afterward, he offered his and his men's services to Andrew Jackson, under the condition that the United States would later pardon them

for their former illegal activities. Badly in need of soldiers, Jackson accepted. At the Battle of New Orleans (January 8, 1815), Laffite and his men fought with distinction, and President Madison later issued them a public pardon. In 1821, Laffite loaded up his belongings and a crew of trusted followers and sailed away. He was never heard from again, so his later life remains as much a mystery as his youth.

Jean Laffite, a unique combination of pirate and patriot, refused to cooperate with the British.

The "Dirty Shirts" Deliver a Night Surprise

Jackson was fortunate that he was able to prepare his defenses so quickly. On the very day that the Tennesseeans rode into New Orleans, the British were fast approaching the city. Admiral Cochrane faced a formidable task in getting his men ashore, for at the time New Orleans was nearly surrounded by swamps and shallow rivers that his large ships could not navigate. So his troops had to row ashore in cutters carrying tons of supplies and weapons, a tedious and difficult endeavor. Undaunted, however, Cochrane moved his cutters back and forth day and night, quickly establishing a base camp on the coast south of the city.

Even before all the troops were ashore, one of Cochrane's officers, General John Keane, led over two thousand of them northward toward New Orleans. He captured a plantation about seven miles outside the city and camped his troops there for the night, confident that the next day he would easily take the town even without the rest of the army. He knew that

BATTLE FOR NEW ORLEANS

Jackson had few regular troops, and he expected token resistance at best from the "inferior" Indians, blacks, and Creoles. Keane also remembered how the Americans had run for their lives at Bladensburg and assured his men that the "dirty shirts" in New Orleans were cowards who would flee just as fast.

When Jackson learned that Keane was camped only seven miles from the city, he smashed his fist into the nearest table. "By the Eternal," he bellowed, "they shall not sleep on our soil!" Acting swiftly, he summoned his officers and told them, "Gentlemen, the British are below [i.e., to the south]. We must fight them tonight."[69] That evening, Old Hickory led about two thousand troops, including some two hundred free blacks and many Creoles, to within a hundred yards of the occupied plantation. Meanwhile, the American gunboat *Carolina* moved silently along a waterway on the other side of the British camp. At Jackson's order, the boat's cannon opened fire, taking Keane and his men completely by surprise. Seconds later, Jackson's forces swarmed into the British camp, initiating a round of savage hand-to-hand combat that went on for almost four hours.

The Americans finally withdrew at about midnight, the casualties being heavy on both sides and there being no way to win a clear-cut victory in the dark. But Jackson's quick action had, as he had hoped it would, gained his forces an important psychological advantage. The shaken British soldiers now saw the "dirty shirts," including the blacks and Creoles, as worthy opponents to be feared and respected. At the same time, Jackson's own forces became more confident. They had proven that they could stand up to, slug it out with, and hold their own against highly trained British regulars, which was no small feat.

The New Year's Artillery Duel

Having tested each other's measure, the two armies prepared for a major confrontation. On Christmas Day 1814, General Edward Pakenham, a veteran of the war with France who had replaced Keane as head of the British ground troops, moved the army's main body northward. Simultaneously, Jackson ordered his own troops to make a stand along a narrow canal a few miles south of New Orleans. Because of the swamps and other natural barriers in the area, the British had to cross the canal to reach the city. The Americans constructed a five-foot-high dirt wall about thirty feet behind the canal and erected wooden platforms atop the wall, on which they placed their cannon. By New Year's Eve, Pakenham had planted dozens of his own cannon several hundred yards directly in front of and facing the American fortifications.

The next morning, January 1, 1815, Pakenham felt he was ready to attack. He planned to use his cannon to blast holes in Jackson's makeshift wall, then march his infantry through the holes. At the British commander's signal, the expert British gunners began blasting away, scoring hits on Jackson's field headquarters, as well as on an American supply boat. The American

Dragging Cannon Through the Swamps

In preparation for the assault on the American position near the canal, General Pakenham ordered that extra cannon be transported from the British beachhead on the coast. In a later report, excerpted here, one of Pakenham's artillery commanders, Captain R. N. Hill, described the operation, providing a vivid illustration of the extreme logistical difficulties encountered by both sides in the war (excerpted from Blaze of Glory).

"The guns and their carriages were brought ashore separately in ships' boats and were then assembled and mounted for transport by land to the position of the Army. . . . Our lack of transport-animals hampered all our efforts. It at once became apparent that our plan of relying on the invaded country for horses or oxen or mules was visionary [imaginary], because all [such animals] belonging to the plantations within our zone of operation had been driven off inside the enemy's fortified lines as soon as our presence [offshore] . . . became known. Under these circumstances, the transport of heavy guns and their ammunition over the Bienvenu road became exceedingly slow and toilsome. In some cases the guns and tumbrils [carriages supporting the cannon] were hauled by the soldiers, manning long drag ropes. The road itself was very bad; passing most of the way through dense cypress swamps, soft and miry everywhere, and frequently 'corduroyed' [consisting of logs laid down in rows]—as the Americans called it—in places where the swamp would otherwise be impassable."

cannon soon answered, scoring hits of their own. After this artillery duel had gone on for almost three hours, Pakenham was disappointed to see that the American positions were still largely intact, so he postponed his all-out attack until he could get more troops from his coastal camp.

It was not until January 8 that Pakenham felt confident that he had sufficient troops in place to overrun the American barricade. At dawn, he fired a rocket, the signal for his officers to move the army forward, and the troops advanced in the open, marching in perfect formation to a beat provided by a long row of drummers. This impractical style of warfare had been traditional in Europe for centuries. But the Americans, as well as the more savvy British commanders in Canada, had abandoned it long ago, viewing it as nothing less than suicidal. This, however, was the way Pakenham had fought Napoleon, and he stubbornly stuck with what he saw as an honorable military tradition.

"Swept from the Face of the Earth"

The Americans stared in stunned disbelief at the advancing British troops, viewing them as little more than sitting ducks. When the enemy was close enough, Jackson ordered his largest cannon to discharge a load of musket balls and scrap metal, and seconds later the rain of fragments tore into the front British ranks, mutilating and flattening over two hundred men at one stroke. Then the other American cannon started blasting away, causing more redcoats to collapse in swathes. Yet despite these losses, the oth-

ers, following their training, stepped over their fallen comrades, closed ranks, and marched mechanically onward in an orderly, disciplined manner.

When the British came within range of the American muskets, the brilliance of Jackson's defensive strategy became apparent. He had lined up his riflemen in four rows, one behind the other; after the men in the front row fired, they moved back, allowing the men in the second row to step forward and fire, and so forth. The resultant continuous volleys were terrifying and lethal. "In less time than one can write it," one American witness later recalled, one large group of redcoats

A bird's-eye view of the Battle of New Orleans shows the British, in neat formation, attacking the American barricades.

was literally swept from the face of the earth. In the wreck and confusion that ensued, within five minutes the regiment seemed to vanish from sight—except the half of it that lay stricken on the ground. Every mounted officer was down at first fire. No such execution by small arms has ever been seen or heard of.[70]

Even then, incredibly, the surviving British soldiers kept coming, trying as best as they could to keep step to those drummers who were left alive and marching resolutely into the deadly hurricane of flying metal. "Never before had British veterans quailed [showed fear]," a British officer later recalled, "but there was something in that leaden torrent that no man on earth could face. In minutes, the entire column was broken and disorganized."[71] Only a handful of the attackers managed to make it to the canal and American barricade. None of them survived the death trap of muskets, pistols, and swords that awaited them. Finally, seeing Pakenham, Keane, and many other officers sprawled dead in the field, another British officer

General Jackson's riflemen fire volley after deadly volley into the approaching British lines, nearly annihilating them.

General Pakenham, who had been confident that his Continental-style battle tactics would prove effective against the "inferior" American forces, is mortally wounded in the attack.

ordered a retreat, ending the slaughter. Shocked and bleeding, the survivors crept away toward the safety of their ships.

A POSITIVE NOTE TO END ON

When the smoke had cleared, it was plain that Jackson had won a victory of epic proportions. The British losses were staggering: 291 dead; 1,262 wounded, many severely; and 484 missing. In comparison, the Americans had lost only 13 dead and 39 wounded. Admiral Cochrane now found himself in a dangerous position. Not only were his casualties horrendous, but the morale of his surviving men had been shattered and his fleet, anchored many miles offshore, could offer no meaningful assistance. Moreover, the Americans were sure to launch a counterattack in full

strength at any moment. There was simply no choice but to withdraw and abandon the expedition, and this he did.

The news of the American victory in New Orleans did not reach the Northeast until well past the middle of January 1815. By that time, the three messengers from the Hartford Convention were in Baltimore. They continued on to Washington, but when they arrived, the city was wildly celebrating the win in the South and no one was in the least interested in their demands. (The butt of insults and ridicule, the three men quietly left town.) In fact, for the next two weeks people all over the country talked of practically nothing else but Jackson's victory and U.S. victories yet to come.

But there would be no more victories. What no one in North America knew at that time was that the war had already

Glorious News
FROM NEW ORLEANS!

Splendid Victory over the British forces!

ESSEX REGISTER OFFICE, Feb. 9.

☞The New-York papers by this morning's mail, furnished us with the following most glorious intelligence from New-Orleans. Gen. JACKSON will be immortalized—the bravery of the Kentuckians, the Tennesseans, &c. shall be handed down to the latest posterity.—If there ever was a stain upon "raw militia," it was wiped away on the 8th of January. The result of this day's contest is of more importance in a national point of view, than any occurrence since the war.

The following is a letter from Mr. Le Blanc, a French merchant at New-Orleans, to a gentleman of New-York.

New-Orleans, Jan. 9—7 P.M.

The battle of the 8th of January was one of the hottest that we have hitherto had, and has happily terminated in our favor. The enemy at break of day appeared in a body principally upon our left, in order to make a passage and turn our line in that direction;—he had for that purpose prepared scaling ladders and fascines to fill up the ditch. For nearly two hours the battle was contested with the greatest fury. The enemy was for five minutes in possession of one of our batteries. Not one of those who attempted the assault escaped—they all fell under our batteries; the plain was strewed with killed and wounded, heaped upon each other. We made

ry their point, but were equally unsuccessful. Such an action the writer thinks, who was present, was never before heard of.

The enemy lost in killed more than 500, wounded brought in by our men near 400.— Those who were only slightly wounded got off to their camp. They lost 40 officers, killed, wounded & prisoners, (20 of them prisoners.) Among the killed was Lieut. Gen. Packenham, Maj Gen. Gibbs, & Gen. Keane badly wounded.

There was not more than 1000 or 1500 of our men engaged. The centre did not fire a shot, and our losing no men it was not requisite for those in the rear to fill up. They were engaged in loading the guns of the front line. So rapid was the enemy's movement, and dark withal, that several of them came within our piquet guards. There was never more determined bravery on both sides than on this occasion. On the opposite side of the river, where we had a small force and a battery, the enemy landed from 4 to 600 men, & by some unaccountable error in our officers, they retreated after spiking their guns.— The enemy however did not long remain, but retreated to the main army again.

Another letter says—Jan. 13,

Their fleet has entered the river, and has been bombarding fort Plaquemine. The result is most anxiously expected.

This broadside from January 8, 1815, celebrates in detail the "Glorious News from New Orleans."

been over for weeks. On February 4, 1815, a ship arrived from Europe with the news that American and British negotiators had signed a peace treaty in the Belgian town of Ghent on Christmas Eve in 1814. This was a full two weeks before the battle at New Orleans. Ironically, then, had the means of communication been quicker, that bloody encounter might have been avoided. Nevertheless, some American leaders privately said they were glad that the battle had been fought, for it had provided a positive note on which to end a long, frustrating, and seemingly unwinnable conflict. On February 17, 1815, President Madison officially announced that the war with Britain was over at last.

The Peace That Came Too Late

The document signed at Ghent ending the War of 1812 was markedly different from most other peace treaties. In the usual scenario, one side in a conflict decisively defeats the other, or one side is unable to continue fighting; the warring parties then sit down to make peace. But when the Treaty of Ghent was signed on December 24, 1814, neither Britain nor the United States had gained complete victory. Moreover, both nations could and did continue fighting for several more weeks.

Actually, the peace talks took place, on and off, all through the war, rather than just near the end of the fighting. Negotiators from the two countries met many times in both England and Belgium, constantly arguing over issues such as shipping rights, Britain's impressment of U.S. sailors, and who should control Indian lands. When news of an American victory reached Europe, the U.S. negotiators bargained, for a time, with a stronger hand. Similarly, news of a British win enabled the other side temporarily to make stronger demands. And as each side tried to establish a clear advantage over the other, the talks dragged on and on.

MOTIVES FOR ENDING THE WAR

What finally persuaded the negotiators to sign the treaty was the realization that for both nations the war was virtually unwinnable. To begin with, it was expensive. Donald Hickey summarizes U.S. expenditures, which were easily matched by those of Britain:

> The cost of the war (excluding property damage and lost economic opportunities) was $158,000,000. This includes $93,000,000 in army and navy expenditures, $16,000,000 for interest on the war loans, and $49,000,000 in veterans' benefits. (The last veteran died in 1905, the last pensioner—the daughter of a veteran, in 1946.) The government also awarded land bounties to some 224,000 people who had served in the war. The national debt, which the Republicans had reduced from $83,000,000 in 1801 to $45,000,000 in 1812, rose to $127,000,000 by the end of 1815.[72]

The fact that both sides' military forces continued to be spread out over vast stretches of land and sea made it certain that expenditures would keep on rising.

The signing of the Treaty of Ghent. Although both the British and the Americans were eager to end hostilities, the treaty did not resolve any of the issues for which the war was fought.

At the same time, this dispersion of the forces rendered prosecuting the conflict difficult for both sides and made it likely that they would continue to rack up fairly equal records of victories and defeats. Considering these realities, by the end of 1814 each side thought it best to salvage whatever it could and get out of the conflict while the getting was good.

This reflected a major change in attitude on the part of the British, who had long been extremely confident of total victory. As noted historian Edwin Hoyt points out, to the British the war "was as a gnat's sting during the long campaign against Napoleon, and for many years the struggle was not even dignified by British history books with a name."[73] Simply put, when they defeated Napoleon and could devote their full attention to fighting the Americans, the British thought victory was assured; because of this, they were unwilling to bargain in the summer of 1814 when their invasion forces were

headed for the United States. Later, however, when their attack on New York fizzled and they were forced to retreat from Baltimore, their only major hope was that Cochrane's forces would be able to capture New Orleans. This would give them control of the Louisiana Territory and a solid and hopefully permanent foothold in North America. Thus, despite recent setbacks, the British signed the treaty confident that Cochrane was already winning; and even after the signing, they authorized sending him reinforcements to help him hold on to the new gains. They clearly intended to put the war behind them and then proceed to develop their new North American colony.

The Americans were also anxious to end the fighting. They had gained control of the Great Lakes and frontier areas, but the Treasury was empty and the army was not large enough to carry on a sustained war. Making matters worse, New England was about to secede, the government was in danger of collapse, and the British were moving on New Orleans. Thus, American negotiators hoped to bring the war to a close before the enemy captured Louisiana and possibly much of the southern United States.

A New American Unity

Since each side had its reasons for ending the conflict, the negotiators finally signed the treaty. However, they still had not resolved the issues over which they had fought the war. The fact is that they could not reach agreement on a single point, so they decided temporarily to ignore their mutual grievances, making the Treaty of Ghent no more than a statement that the countries would, at least for the moment, cease hostilities. There was no mention of shipping rights, impressment, Indian issues, or territorial gains for either nation. The parties stated their intentions to discuss and hopefully to resolve these issues in future meetings. But for the moment

In this nineteenth-century engraving, the end of the War of 1812 is depicted in grand terms. In reality, there was no overall victory for either side.

they preferred to maintain what they called the *status quo ante bellum*, or "situation that existed before the war."

Of course, as they signed the treaty the negotiators on both sides believed that the British would likely capture Louisiana. Soon, however, Andrew Jackson's unexpected and decisive victory came to overshadow the treaty itself and became, in everyone's minds, the real conclusion of the war. It was, therefore, Jackson's win, and not the treaty, that actually ended British dreams of an empire in North America. To many British, the battle was a tragic waste that might have been avoided if news of peace had not arrived too late.

By contrast, most Americans thought that the victory in New Orleans was a confirmation that they had won the war. The news from Louisiana spread across the country nearly a month before the news from Ghent arrived, so the vast majority of people mistakenly thought that Jackson's victory had forced the British to sign the treaty. In reality, of course, there was no clear-cut winner. At the war's end, the biggest successes the United States could claim were that it had lost no territory and that its government had not collapsed.

Yet Jackson's stunning victory instilled a new sense of pride in the American people. There was a widespread feeling

As the British charge in orderly columns, American soldiers fire cannon and muskets straight into their lines during the Battle of New Orleans.

that they had overcome British tyranny a second time, and a surge of patriotism gripped the country and brought a sense of unity that had been lacking for many years. American diplomat Albert Gallatin summed up the new national attitude, saying, "The war has renewed . . . the national feelings and character which the Revolution had given. . . . The people . . . are more American; they feel and act more as a nation."[74]

One important effect of this new unity was the end it brought to some long-standing political squabbles. Most people now agreed that the needs of the country as a whole should come before the needs of individual states, so New England's complaints and demands suddenly seemed petty and its leaders disloyal. In contrast, respect for the federal government increased, and future presidents would find it easier to unite the country in time of danger.

BOTH SIDES LEARN HARD LESSONS

Another outcome of the War of 1812 was that it taught both the British and Americans important lessons about waging war. Britain, a world-class power, had been unable to subdue the far less powerful United States, as many observers around the world had expected would occur. This was partly because of Britain's attempt to fight the French and Americans at the same time; for most of the war, the British could not devote adequate troops and supplies to the North American conflict,

which gave the Americans time to expand and improve their own army. Also, on the whole the British assigned their best generals to fight against Napoleon. Most of the British leaders in America lacked skill, imagination, and daring and, moreover, were overconfident, often assuming that the Americans were completely undisciplined and unskilled. It was this short-sighted attitude that led to Captain Dacres' loss of the *Guerriere* and General Pakenham's defeat in New Orleans.

The Americans learned a lesson about overconfidence as well. The war hawks declared war believing that invading and conquering Canada would be an easy affair; and William Hull lost Detroit because he expected the British to retreat at the first sight of an American army. Fortunately for the Americans, this attitude changed during the course of the war. Clearly, part of what made Oliver Perry and Andrew Jackson effective leaders was their respect for the enemy's ability.

Perhaps the most important military lesson the Americans learned was to be prepared. At the outset of the fighting, the country's army was much too small to fight a major war, the troops had little training, and the generals were inexperienced. In addition, the navy lacked firepower and sufficient vessels to defend thousands of miles of coastline. After the war, the state of the military became more of a national priority. "Experience has taught us," President Madison remarked to Congress while announcing the war's end, "that a certain degree of preparation for war is not only indispensable to avert disasters in the onset, but affords also

The USS Constitution, *pride of the American navy, undergoes a major overhaul and refitting later in the nineteenth century.*

the best security for the continuance of peace."[75] Agreeing with him, in 1815 and 1816 Congress authorized funds for the maintenance of a peacetime standing army of ten thousand men (three times the size of the 1801 army); the construction of twenty-one new warships; and the start of an ambitious program to fortify the coasts. Never again would the United States be so unprepared to defend itself.

WEALTH, EXPANSION, AND NEWFOUND RESPECT

Another outcome of the war consisted of a different kind of U.S. military expansion, one that would have important con-

sequences for the nation's future. This was its development of the beginnings of a major weapons industry. Before the war, many of the arms used by U.S. troops came from other countries; however, the British Orders in Council, which limited U.S. shipping, had deprived the Americans of these foreign weapons. Accordingly, American engineers and artisans rose to the challenge, managing to produce all the muskets, cannon, and gunpowder needed to wage the war. U.S. manufacturing plants grew in size and number, and American companies even began selling weapons to other countries. The United States has been one of the world's foremost arms suppliers ever since.

This increase in manufacturing greatly boosted the country's economy, which in turn sparked more industrial growth and over time helped to make the United States a wealthy nation. Also adding to the country's wealth were the lands taken from the Indians during the war. White settlers' contempt for Indians increased in these years partly because so many tribes allied themselves with the British; consequently, afterward it became more acceptable to many Americans to kill Indians and confiscate their lands. Many of the seized Creek territories became rich southern cotton plantations. And the Indian lands of the Ohio Valley became farms, eventually part of the vast midwestern

"breadbasket" that would feed the nation's growing population. The frontier yielded large amounts of valuable furs, timber, and precious metals.

The control of the frontier gained during the war also allowed the United States to begin a rapid process of westward expansion, a movement that would prove unstoppable and end only when the country stretched from the Atlantic to the Pacific. "With the Indian dangers gone and foreign influence dissipated, the rich agricultural regions beckoned," writes Marquette University scholar Francis Prucha, "and the tide of emigrants, dammed up for a decade, poured out over the land. Within five years after the

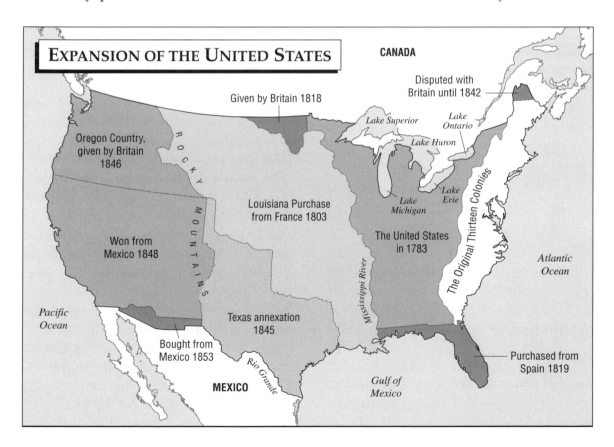

EXPANSION OF THE UNITED STATES

CANADA

Given by Britain 1818

Disputed with Britain until 1842

Lake Superior

Lake Ontario

Lake Huron

Oregon Country, given by Britain 1846

ROCKY MOUNTAINS

Louisiana Purchase from France 1803

Lake Michigan

Lake Erie

The United States in 1783

The Original Thirteen Colonies

Atlantic Ocean

Won from Mexico 1848

Pacific Ocean

Mississippi River

Texas annexation 1845

Bought from Mexico 1853

Rio Grande

MEXICO

Gulf of Mexico

Purchased from Spain 1819

War of 1812, five new western states entered the Union."[76] In these years and those that followed, many Americans came to believe that it was their destiny to control the frontier, and they looked on other nations and peoples holding lands within it as intruders. Throughout the nineteenth century, the United States, either by war or negotiation, absorbed huge territories belonging to Spain, Mexico, France, Britain, and numerous Native American tribes.

One more important legacy of the war and the U.S. military and territorial expansion that it generated cannot be overlooked. This was the enhanced respect the nation gained in the eyes of the great European powers. "The war has raised our reputation in Europe," declared U.S. peace commissioner James Bayard in December 1814, "and it excites astonishment that we should have been able . . . to have fought Great Britain single handed. . . . I think it will be a long time before we are disturbed again by any of the powers of Europe."[77] Indeed, Professor Hickey adds,

> The British were [thereafter] careful not to impress any Americans. . . . In fact, Americans were never again subjected to those dubious maritime practices that had caused the war. With Europe generally at peace in the [nineteenth] century, the Great Powers had no interest in regulating American trade or in tampering with the nation's merchant marine. The United States had ample time to grow and to husband its strength.[78]

TWO ULTIMATE WINNERS

It should be emphasized that the most important reason that the United States enjoyed the luxury of being left alone to develop its strength and resources was the friendship that grew between the Americans and British in the decades following the War of 1812. After the conflict, Britain stopped seeing its former enemy as a country of rebels with little chance for success. The British finally accepted the United States as a permanent nation, one that could be a valuable ally and trading partner. And in fact, the flourishing trade that quickly developed between the two countries greatly benefited Britain's economy and helped it to maintain its huge worldwide empire. In return, Britain provided the protection of its still great navy. Its almost complete domination of the seas ensured that no other European powers could extend their influence into North America. This guaranteed the United States a century of unlimited growth, secure from the threat of foreign intervention.

Most significant of all, both the Americans and the British eventually regarded the differences they had fought over as minor disputes. They signed agreements settling these disputes and began to build a positive and lasting friendship. In time, this course of events seemed only natural, for, after all, the two countries had a great deal in common. They shared the same language and heritage, as well as similar laws, customs, and ideas. The mighty alliance forged between the two peoples eventually helped shape the course of world history, as Americans and British

British and American allies joyfully embrace one another on hearing of their total victory over Germany at the conclusion of World War II. The permanent friendship of the two nations was ultimately the most important outcome of the 1812 conflict.

fought side by side making the world safe for freedom and democracy during the devastating world wars of the twentieth century.

The most important outcome of the war, then, was that the combatants quickly put their differences behind them. The Treaty of Ghent had come too late to prevent the slaughter in New Orleans. But it was a peace that would endure for centuries. And though no decisive victor emerged from the conflict, it later became plain that the act of becoming friends and allies made both nations decided winners.

Notes

Introduction: A War Scarcely Anyone Wanted

1. Quoted in Irwin Unger, *These United States: The Questions of Our Past*, vol. 1, *To 1877*. Boston: Little, Brown, 1978, p. 222.

2. Quoted in Reginald Horsman, *The War of 1812*. New York: Knopf, 1969, p. 24.

3. Pierre Berton, *The Invasion of Canada*, vol. 1, *1812–1813*. Boston: Little, Brown, 1980, p. 314.

4. Donald R. Hickey, *The War of 1812: A Forgotten Conflict*. Chicago: University of Illinois Press, 1989, p. 2.

5. Introduction to George R. Taylor, ed., *The War of 1812: Past Justifications and Present Interpretations*. Boston: D. C. Heath, 1963, p. v.

Chapter 1: Down the Fateful Road to War

6. Quoted in Allan W. Eckert, *The Frontiersmen: A Narrative*. Boston: Little, Brown, 1967, pp. 314–15.

7. March 10, 1812, issue, quoted in William S. Dudley, ed., *The Naval War of 1812: A Documentary History*. 3 vols. Washington, DC: Naval Historical Center, Dept. of the Navy, 1985–1992, vol. 1, pp. 62–63.

8. Quoted in Eckert, *The Frontiersmen*, p. 532.

9. December 7, 1811, issue, quoted in Bradford Perkins, *Prologue to War: England and the United States, 1805–1812*. Berkeley and Los Angeles: University of California Press, 1968, p. 284.

10. December 10, 1811, issue, quoted in Perkins, *Prologue to War*, p. 284.

11. Quoted in Taylor, *The War of 1812*, pp. 28–29, 32.

Chapter 2: The Disastrous Canadian Campaign

12. John R. Elting, *Amateurs, to Arms! A Military History of the War of 1812*. Chapel Hill, NC: Algonquin Books, 1991, pp. 23–24.

13. Russell F. Weigley, *History of the United States Army*. New York: Macmillan, 1967, pp. 115–16.

14. Weigley, *History of the United States Army*, p. 124.

15. Weigley, *History of the United States Army*, p. 115.

16. Quoted in Harry L. Coles, *The War of 1812*. Chicago: University of Chicago Press, 1965, p. 45.

17. Quoted in Coles, *War of 1812*, p. 52.

18. Quoted in Coles, *War of 1812*, p. 53.

19. Quoted in Eckert, *The Frontiersmen*, p. 546.

20. Quoted in Henry Adams, *The War of 1812*, ed. H. A. De Weerd. Washington, DC: Infantry Journal Press, 1944, p. 24.

21. Noted Canadian historian Pierre Berton points out the ironic likelihood that had Hull "refused to surrender, had he gone down to defeat, his fort and town shattered by cannon fire, his friends and neighbors savaged by the misfortunes of battle, his soldiers dead to the last man . . . the tired old general would have swept into the history books as a gallant martyr, his name enshrined on bridges, schools, main streets, and public buildings." (*The Invasion of Canada*, vol. 1, p. 188).

22. Robert Leckie, *The Wars of America*. New York: Harper and Row, 1968, p. 246.

Chapter 3: Victories on the Open Sea

23. Dudley W. Knox, *A History of the United States Navy*. New York: Putnam, 1936, p.82.

The United States also had upwards of two hundred "gunboats," small vessels that carried one or two cannon and some soldiers with muskets. These were no match for even the smallest warships and were used only for defensive purposes inside shallow harbors.

24. Quoted in Dudley, *The Naval War of 1812,* vol. 1, pp. 135–36.

25. Quoted in Dudley, *The Naval War of 1812,* vol. 1, p. 162.

26. Tyrone G. Martin, *A Most Fortunate Ship: A Narrative History of "Old Ironsides."* Chester, CT: Globe Pequot Press, 1980, p. 107.

27. Quoted in Dudley, *The Naval War of 1812,* vol. 1, p. 165.

28. Quoted in James Barnes, *Naval Actions of the War of 1812.* New York: Harper and Brothers, 1896, p. 32.

29. Martin, *A Most Fortunate Ship,* p. 109.

30. Quoted in Albert Marrin, *1812: The War Nobody Won.* New York: Atheneum, 1985, p. 59.

31. Quoted in Martin, *A Most Fortunate Ship,* p. 117.

32. Quoted in Martin, *A Most Fortunate Ship,* pp. 122–23. It should be emphasized that Hull first made preparations to tow the *Guerriere* to port, but when his men informed him that the water level in its flooded hold was five feet and rising, he felt there was no choice but to destroy it.

33. Quoted in Horsman, *War of 1812,* p. 62.

34. Quoted in Leckie, *Wars of America,* p. 250.

35. Quoted in Leckie, *Wars of America,* p. 251.

Chapter 4: Battle for the Great Lakes

36. Elting, *Amateurs, to Arms!* p. 87.

37. Quoted in Coles, *War of 1812,* p. 121.

38. Quoted in Hickey, *War of 1812,* p. 155. "Don't give up the ship" subsequently became the proud motto of the U.S. Navy.

39. Quoted in Leckie, *Wars of America,* p. 55.

40. Quoted in Dudley, *The Naval War of 1812,* vol. 2, p. 530. Chauncey was insulted by Perry's complaint and also by the younger officer's tendency to communicate directly with the navy secretary, thereby bypassing Chauncey in the chain of command. On July 30, Chauncey wrote to Perry expressing his displeasure. See pp. 529–33 for sample letters passed between Perry, Chauncey, and the navy secretary.

41. Quoted in Dudley, *The Naval War of 1812,* vol. 2, p. 559.

42. Quoted in Dudley, *The Naval War of 1812,* vol. 2, p. 553.

Chapter 5: Mortal Combat on the Frontier

43. John Sugden, *Tecumseh's Last Stand.* Norman: University of Oklahoma Press, 1985, p. 17.

44. Quoted in Sugden, *Tecumseh's Last Stand,* pp. 54–55.

45. Quoted in Sugden, *Tecumseh's Last Stand,* p. 55.

46. Quoted in Eckert, *The Frontiersmen,* p. 580.

47. Quoted in Eckert, *The Frontiersmen,* pp. 581–82.

48. Quoted in Eckert, *The Frontiersmen,* p. 582.

49. Quoted in Sugden, *Tecumseh's Last Stand,* p. 126.

50. Proctor was later tried by a Montreal military court and found guilty of several counts of poor judgment or conduct in the days preceding, as well as during, the Thames battle; as a sentence he received a public reprimand and temporary demotion in rank and loss of pay.

51. Quoted in Hickey, *War of 1812,* p. 149.

52. Samuel E. Morison, *The Oxford History of the American People.* New York: Oxford University Press, 1965, p. 391.

53. Quoted in Hickey, *War of 1812,* p. 182.

Chapter 6: Washington in Flames

54. Quoted in Robert Leckie, *The War Nobody Won: 1812.* New York: Putnam, 1974, p. 113.

55. Quoted in Walter Lord, *The Dawn's Early Light.* New York: W. W. Norton, 1972, p. 33.

56. The original plan called for an attack on the lakes region, but this was vetoed because of the strong American naval presence on the lakes.

57. Quoted in Leckie, *Wars of America,* p. 284.

58. Quoted in Irving Brant, *The Fourth President: A Life of James Madison.* New York: Bobbs-Merrill, 1970, p. 572.

59. Quoted in Leckie, *Wars of America,* p. 290.

60. Quoted in Hickey, *War of 1812,* p. 198.

61. When news of the senseless destruction of the library reached London, many British were horrified and demanded that their government apologize. Later, Thomas Jefferson sold his private book collection to the government to create the nucleus of a new national library, which today contains over 80 million books and other items.

62. Quoted in Brant, *The Fourth President,* p. 574.

63. The song did not receive the title "Star-Spangled Banner" until several years later. Congress adopted it as the national anthem on March 3, 1931.

Chapter 7: Triumph in New Orleans

64. Quoted in Brant, *The Fourth President,* p. 582.

65. Quoted in Brant, *The Fourth President,* p. 582.

66. Quoted in Samuel Carter III, *Blaze of Glory: The Fight for New Orleans, 1814–1815.* New York: St. Martin's Press, 1971, p. 100.

67. Quoted in Carter, *Blaze of Glory,* p. 45.

68. Quoted in Leckie, *War Nobody Won,* p. 141.

69. Quoted in Leckie, *Wars of America,* p. 305.

70. Quoted in Carter, *Blaze of Glory,* p. 254.

71. Quoted in Carter, *Blaze of Glory,* pp. 255–56.

Epilogue: The Peace That Came Too Late

72. Hickey, *War of 1812,* p. 303.

73. Edwin P. Hoyt, *America's Wars and Military Excursions.* New York: McGraw-Hill, 1987, p. 136.

74. Quoted in Unger, *These United States,* pp. 229–30.

75. Quoted in Hickey, *War of 1812,* p. 304.

76. Francis P. Prucha, *The Sword of the Republic: The United States Army on the Frontier, 1783–1846.* New York: Macmillan, 1969, p. 119.

77. Quoted in Lord, *Dawn's Early Light,* p. 342.

78. Hickey, *War of 1812,* p. 307.

For Further Reading

Alden R. Carter, *The War of 1812: Second Fight for Independence.* New York: Franklin Watts, 1992. A well-written basic introduction to the war.

Henry E. Gruppe, *The Frigates.* Alexandria, VA: Time-Life Books, 1979. Like other entries from the Time-Life series, this one, about the sailing ships that plied the waves in the eighteenth and nineteenth centuries, is informative, beautifully illustrated, and written clearly enough to appeal to general readers both young and old.

Robert Leckie, *Great American Battles.* New York: Random House, 1968. Leckie, a distinguished historian, does a fine job here describing for a junior-high audience the backgrounds and outcomes of several famous American battles. Includes a chapter on Andrew Jackson's victory over the British at New Orleans, one of the major events of the War of 1812.

Robert M. Quackenbush, *James Madison and Dolley Madison and Their Times.* New York: Pippin Press, 1992. A handsomely mounted little book that provides young people with a brief but colorful glimpse of the United States in the early nineteenth century.

Patricia R. Quiri, *The National Anthem.* Danbury, CT: Childrens Press, 1998. A comprehensive overview of the "Star-Spangled Banner," including its conception by Francis Scott Key at the height of the British bombardment of Fort McHenry during the War of 1812.

Russell Shorto, *Tecumseh and the Dream of an American Indian Nation.* Englewood Cliffs, NJ: Silver Burdett, 1989. This well-mounted introduction to the great Indian leader who died during the War of 1812 will appeal to basic and intermediate readers.

Robert Tallant, *The Pirate Lafitte and the Battle of New Orleans.* New York: Random House, 1951. A commendable overview of the closing events of the War of 1812, written for young people.

Irwin Unger, *These United States: The Questions of Our Past.* Vol. 1, *To 1877.* Boston: Little, Brown, 1978. Superior of its kind, this general introduction to American history has a comprehensive and clearly written text, as well as several interesting and relevant sidebars and many drawings, photos, and maps.

David Weitzman, *Old Ironsides: Americans Build a Fighting Ship.* Boston: Houghton Mifflin, 1997. A well-written and handsomely illustrated description of the famous USS *Constitution* and how it was created. Aimed at grade school readers.

Major Works Consulted

Pierre Berton, *The Invasion of Canada.* Vol. 1, *1812–1813.* Boston: Little, Brown, 1980. One of Canada's most popular writers presents an informative, lively telling of the failed U.S. attempt to bring Canada into the American fold during the War of 1812, which he calls "a foolish war that scarcely anyone wanted."

Irving Brant, *The Fourth President: A Life of James Madison.* New York: Bobbs-Merrill, 1970. This is a one-volume distillation (but still substantial at more than six hundred pages) of Brant's monumental, widely acclaimed six-volume study of Madison's life. Contains much useful information about American leaders' motivations, debates, decisions, and other behind-the-scenes activity during the War of 1812.

Samuel Carter III, *Blaze of Glory: The Fight for New Orleans, 1814–1815.* New York: St. Martin's Press, 1971. A detailed, absorbing telling of the War of 1812's southern theater of operations, including Andrew Jackson's major victory over the British in a battle unknowingly fought after the conflict had ended.

William S. Dudley, ed., *The Naval War of 1812: A Documentary History.* 3 vols. Washington, DC: Naval Historical Center, Dept. of the Navy, 1985–1992. These three large volumes are crammed full of original letters and other valuable primary-source documents relating to naval operations during the war. Also informative and useful are Dudley's introductory pieces and other commentary and his detailed footnotes and other documentation. An invaluable source for serious students of the conflict.

John R. Elting, *Amateurs, to Arms! A Military History of the War of 1812.* Chapel Hill, NC: Algonquin Books, 1991. An excellent, detailed study of the war's battles, leaders, and strategies, by a distinguished military historian.

Donald R. Hickey, *The War of 1812: A Forgotten Conflict.* Chicago: University of Illinois Press, 1989. A detailed, well-informed narrative of the war, packed with information about economic and social, as well as political and military, issues. Highly recommended.

Robert Leckie, *The Wars of America.* New York: Harper and Row, 1968. This excellent historical overview of the wars fought by the United States from colonial days up to the first years of the Vietnam conflict contains the best concise synopsis of the War of 1812 (pp. 219–313) that I am aware of. Highly recommended.

Walter Lord, *The Dawn's Early Light.* New York: W. W. Norton, 1972. A fine, prolific historian's rousing and well-documented telling of the last phase of the War of 1812.

Tyrone G. Martin, *A Most Fortunate Ship: A Narrative History of "Old Ironsides."* Chester, CT: Globe Pequot Press, 1980. This well-written history of the most famous U.S. warship contains an extensive synopsis (pp. 89–168) of the vessel's service in the War of 1812, including the famous "Great Chase," in which, under the command of the talented and resourceful Isaac Hull, it outmaneuvered and outran an entire squadron of British warships.

Bradford Perkins, *Prologue to War: England and the United States, 1805–1812.* Berkeley and Los Angeles: University of California Press, 1968. A very detailed scholarly study of the social, economic, political, and diplomatic events and trends that led up to the outbreak of the War of 1812.

Tim Pickles, *New Orleans, 1815: Andrew Jackson Crushes the British.* London: Osprey, 1993. Part of Osprey's excellent series on historical military campaigns and battles, this is a detailed, colorful examination of the Battle of New Orleans, with an informative text and numerous maps and illustrations.

John Sugden, *Tecumseh's Last Stand.* Norman: University of Oklahoma Press, 1985. This comprehensive overview of the U.S. campaign against the British and Indians in the Old Northwest in 1813 details Tecumseh's goals, achievements, and ultimate death in battle during the War of 1812. The book also paints a vivid picture of the era and the motivations behind the fighting.

Russell F. Weigley, *History of the United States Army.* New York: Macmillan, 1967. A masterful scholarly work detailing the enlistment issues and practices, supplies, officers, training, readiness, methods, and other aspects of the development and evolution of U.S. land forces.

Additional Works Consulted

Henry Adams, *The War of 1812.* Ed. H. A. De Weerd. Washington, DC: Infantry Journal Press, 1944.

Gardner W. Allen, ed., *Papers of Isaac Hull, Commodore United States Navy.* Boston: Atheneum, 1929.

James Barnes, *Naval Actions of the War of 1812.* New York: Harper and Brothers, 1896.

Roger H. Brown, *The Republic in Peril: 1812.* New York: Columbia University Press, 1964.

David Colbert, ed., *Eyewitness to America: 500 Years of America in the Words of Those Who Saw It Happen.* New York: Pantheon Books, 1997.

Harry L. Coles, *The War of 1812.* Chicago: University of Chicago Press, 1965.

George W. Cullum, *Campaigns of the War of 1812.* New York: J. Miller, 1979.

Richard Dillon, *We Have Met the Enemy: Oliver Hazard Perry, Wilderness Commander.* New York: McGraw-Hill, 1978.

Allan W. Eckert, *The Frontiersmen: A Narrative.* Boston: Little, Brown, 1967.

C. S. Forester, *The Age of Sail: The Story of the Naval War of 1812.* Garden City, NY: Doubleday, 1956.

John Gellner, ed., *Recollections of the War of 1812: Three Eyewitness Accounts.* Toronto: Baxter, 1964.

Donald E. Graves, *The Battle of Lundy's Lane: On the Niagara in 1814.* Baltimore: Nautical and Aviation Press, 1993.

———, ed., *Merry Hearts Make Light Days: The War of 1812 Journal of Lieutenant John Le Couteur, 104th Foot.* Ottawa: Carleton University Press, 1994.

Donald R. Hickey, *The War of 1812: A Short History.* Chicago: University of Illinois Press, 1995.

Reginald Horsman, *The War of 1812.* New York: Knopf, 1969.

Edwin P. Hoyt, *America's Wars and Military Excursions.* New York: McGraw-Hill, 1987.

Dudley W. Knox, *A History of the United States Navy.* New York: Putnam, 1936.

Robert Leckie, *The War Nobody Won: 1812.* New York: Putnam, 1974.

A. T. Mahan, *Sea Power in Its Relations to the War of 1812.* 2 vols. New York: Greenwood Press, 1968.

Albert Marrin, *1812: The War Nobody Won.* New York: Atheneum, 1985.

Samuel E. Morison, *The Oxford History of the American People.* New York: Oxford University Press, 1965.

Charles G. Muller, *The Proudest Day: Macdonough on Lake Champlain.* New York: John Day, 1960.

———, *The Darkest Day: 1814, the Washington-Baltimore Campaign.* Philadelphia: J. B. Lippincott, 1963.

Geofferey Perret, *A Country Made by War: From the Revolution to Viet-Nam—the Story of America's Rise to Power.* New York: Random House, 1989.

Francis P. Prucha, *The Sword of the Republic: The United States Army on the Frontier, 1783–1846.* New York: Macmillan, 1969.

Robert V. Remini, *Andrew Jackson and the Course of American Empire, 1767–1821.* New York: Harper and Row, 1977.

Robert B. Roberts, *Encyclopedia of Historic Forts.* New York: Macmillan, 1988.

J. C. A. Stag, *Mr. Madison's War.* Princeton, NJ: Princeton University Press, 1983.

Suzanne J. Stark, *Female Tars: Women Aboard Ship in the Age of Sail.* Annapolis, MD: Naval Institute Press, 1996.

George R. Taylor, ed., *The War of 1812: Past Justifications and Present Interpretations.* Boston: D. C. Heath, 1963.

Glenn Tucker, *Tecumseh: The Vision of Glory.* New York: Russell and Russell, 1973.

Joseph A. Whitehorne, *While Washington Burned: The Battle of Fort Erie.* Baltimore: Nautical and Aviation Press, 1992.

Index

Picture Credits

Cover photo: AKG Photo, London

Corbis, 12, 43, 111

Corbis/Philip Gould, 93

Corbis/The Mariners' Museum, 108

Corbis/Lee Snider, 11, 72

Corbis-Bettmann, 20, 63, 71, 90

Digital Stock, 58

Dover Publications, Incorporated, 33

Illinois State Historical Library, 69

Library of Congress, 15, 16, 17, 23 (left), 24, 31, 42, 45, 49, 50, 51 (both), 52, 60, 61, 62, 65, 75, 77, 78, 79, 80, 84, 85, 89, 91, 99, 100, 102, 104, 105, 106

Lineworks, Incorporated, 14, 38, 47, 55, 59, 82, 96, 109

The National Portrait Gallery, Smithsonian Institution, 32, 57, 73

North Wind Picture Archives, 18, 23 (right), 29, 87

Prints Old & Rare, 25

© Smithsonian Institution, 39

© Stock Montage, Inc., 19, 36, 37, 95, 101

About the Author

Historian and award-winning author Don Nardo has written many books for young adults about American history and government, including *The U.S. Presidency, The Mexican American War, The Declaration of Independence, The Bill of Rights, The Great Depression*, and *Franklin D. Roosevelt: U.S. President*. Mr. Nardo has also written several teleplays and screenplays, including work for Warner Brothers and ABC-Television. He lives with his wife, Christine, and dog, Bud, on Cape Cod, Massachusetts.